BRAVE

12 Projects Inspired by 20th-Century Art

NEW

From Art Nouveau to Punk & Pop

QUILTS

Kathreen Ricketson

stashBOOKS®

an imprint of C&T Publishing

Text copyright © 2013 by Kathreen Ricketson

Photography and Artwork copyright © 2013 by C&T Publishing, Inc.

Publisher: Amy Marson

Creative Director: Gailen Runge

Art Director/Book Designer: Kristy Zacharias

Editor: Liz Aneloski

Technical Editors: Julie Waldman and Gailen Runge

Production Coordinator: Jenny Davis

Production Editors: Joanna Burgarino and Katie Van Amburg

Illustrator: Robert Shugg

Style Photography: Lee Grant, unless otherwise noted

Quilt Photography: Mark Heriot, unless otherwise noted

Inspiration Boards and Fabrics: Kathreen Ricketson, unless otherwise noted

Published by Stash Books, an imprint of C&T Publishing, Inc., P.O. Box 1456, Lafayette, CA 94549

Library of Congress Cataloging-in-Publication Data

Ricketson, Kathreen.

 Brave new quilts : 12 projects inspired by 20th-century art - from art nouveau to punk & pop / Kathreen Ricketson.

  pages cm

 ISBN 978-1-60705-719-2 (soft cover)

 1. Quilting--Patterns. 2. Art, Modern--20th century--Influence. I. Title.

 TT835.R5363 2013

 746.46--dc23

                        2012046259

Printed in China

10 9 8 7 6 5 4 3 2 1

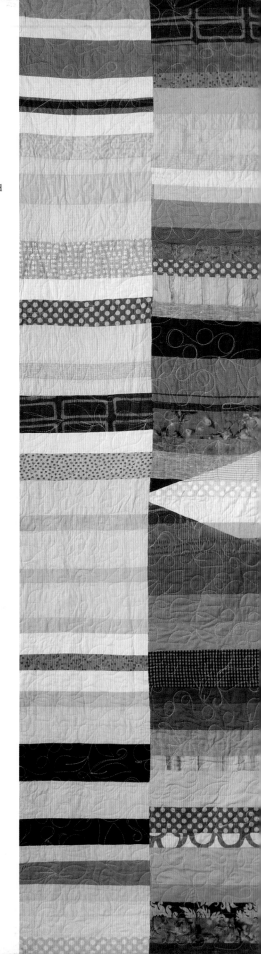

Dedication

For my family—I love you guys—always and forever.

CONTENTS

Acknowledgments

Big giant kisses and hugs to my husband and best friend, Rob Shugg—he keeps me on track, gives me space and time to create, and supports all my schemes and ideas. For this book in particular, he acted as technical assistant to my longarm quilting machine, studio helper in cutting strips of fabric, and illustrator in creating all the illustrations for this book (on top of taking on extra kid and cooking duties, too—he is a star!).

More kisses and more hugs to my two creative munchkins, Otilija and Orlando—their spontaneous creativity keeps me energized. They offer advice on color and design and are incredibly understanding of my deadlines that involve my spending more time with my sewing machine than with them.

I also must thank my friend Julie MacMahon for acting as studio helper and design consultant; she is also the sewing star who sewed the *Bright Future* (page 88) quilt top. Thank you to my quilty neighbor Chris Hayes for letting me rummage in her fabric stash, and thank you to Moda for sending me a few fabric samples to play with and use in some of the quilts here and there.

Thanks to the team at Stash Books for believing in this book and to my agent, Courtney Miller-Callihan, for her continued advice and for helping to make it all happen. Lovely thanks to Mark Heriot for his help with the flat shots of the quilts. Big thanks to Lee Grant, who took the beautiful styled photographs; to Tania, Donna, and Jill, who lent us their homes; and to the beautiful Ella and Otilija, the handsome Orlando, and the patient pets who appear in the book.

Thank you heaps to Susan Boden for writing such a thoughtful foreword for this book and to all my blog readers, newsletter subscribers, Twitter followers, Facebook fans, Flickr groupies, and fellow bloggers and online crafty pals. You all raise me up and make me a better crafter, better writer, better photographer, and all-around better person. I would not have found crafting as a career if were not for you!

Foreword

No one single English word describes Kathreen Ricketson. Her art, her work, her life, her home—these all make her. But however important each word is, Kathreen cannot be reduced to a few English vowels and consonants. Part urban homesteader, part Web 2.0 creator, and fully herself, Kathreen always has her eye on experimentation and pushing the expression of her art. To describe her properly, we need a language that makes a single word from butting other words against each other. Stand back and you see how the fragments connect and morph to form a unified whole of complex, interacting parts. *Gesamtkunstwerk* is such a word and describes Kathreen and this new book, *Brave New Quilts*.

Formed from three German words—*Gesamt* (the whole), *Kunst* (fine art), and *Werk* (work)—Gesamtkunstwerk literally means a total work of art. At first, the word was used to describe the supernatural and mystical nature of art that came as creators worked their abstract imagination and formed a piece of art. By the mid-twentieth century—and especially in architecture—the word described a unity of creation where the architect controlled the building, interior, landscape, and furnishings. Nature, industry, and art, it was argued, should be expressed in a unified harmony. The architect should have the capacities of artist, technician, and artisan.

It is no coincidence that this book focuses on modern art movements as an imaginative springboard to Kathreen's textiles. The German Bauhaus is the natural twentieth-century home for this very-twenty-first-century maker. Founded in 1919, the Bauhaus rose from the shards of World War I as a reaction to the romanticism and excessive ornament of the previous age. Instead, a "new objectivity" was encouraged, where function related to the designed form. The machine age had begun, and like the manager who controlled the new industrial production lines, the architect was the omnipotent creator, skilled in design, materials, and construction.

The quilts in this book draw on a breadth of modern art movements. Some, like *Peacock Blue* (page 98) and *Seedpod* (page 106), are close to their original inspiration in nature. Others, like *Bright Future* (page 88) and *Rhythm* (page 56), capture the energy and hope of an age urgent for its future. And *Break the Rules* (page 122) and *Frothy Nothing* (page 114) free words just

as punk and Dada did at opposite ends of the twentieth century. Like the movements that inspire this book, Kathreen wants you to free your inventiveness and embrace the integrity and clarity you have as a maker of a work of art.

Just as you think carefully about your materials and techniques, wondering how your hands and machines can work your imagination into reality, Kathreen is doing the same. If you strive to create a continuity between the many versions of yourself that modernity imposes, Kathreen is walking that road too. Just like the architects of the Bauhaus, Kathreen is designing, reflecting, and experimenting and, through her books, blog, and textiles, is in dialogue with us all.

And even if that long German word and the cultural history it carries seem a little off-putting, just imagine it in a different way—a bold appliqué stretching across one of Kathreen's quilts. The curves of the S, the vigor of the K, the harmony of the U. Gesamtkunstwerk—this word alone tells you the value of *Brave New Quilts*.

Dr. Susan Boden
Quilter, Whipup Fan, Landscape Architect
Canberra, Australia, July 2012

INTRO-DUCTION

My own personal aesthetic is hard to pin down—modern/retro perhaps or contemporary/traditional—and that fusion of opposites is what I love when designing.

I am deeply attracted to the natural world, organic shapes, and interesting motifs, which is probably why I love midcentury textiles so much. At the same time I admire clean lines and unusual color combinations (punk and pop culture can teach us a lot about new ways of looking at color). I am interested in pattern—intersections of shapes, grids, and linear design (one of the reasons I love Russian constructivist fabrics). This book challenged me to bring these different ideas, elements, and artistic concepts together and to set them within the boundaries of a beautiful and cohesive design. Combing through all of my designs, you will notice a little spark of quirkiness as I show my love of the unusual, clever, and fun.

A major aspect of my quiltmaking style is to keep it simple. These are not hand-pieced, hand-appliquéd quilts made by artisans and traditionalists; there is a place for those, but it is not in this book. Here I want to inspire you to design your own quilt, to be confident with color, not to be too precious about perfection, to take some design and color risks, and above all else to be proud of your work.

When I say "don't be precious" about perfection, I don't mean that you can be sloppy and lazy; you should always be trying to improve your skills and learning new ways of doing things. Of course, it is important to take pride in your work, but you shouldn't avoid trying something new just because you are afraid of failure. It is much better to aim for perfection and only get to 70 percent than to not try at all.

In this vein I think that beginner quilters with some sewing experience should be able to tackle all of the quilts in this book. If you have never sewn before, then you'll need to first get some sewing experience under your belt. Get to know your sewing machine and your tools, and learn some sewing basics. Start with some simple sewing projects before making the quilts in this book. However, if you can sew a bag or a skirt or a cushion, I think you can sew a quilt. If you are an intermediate or even an advanced quilter, you will certainly have a lot fun making and remixing the designs in this book.

If you love color and pattern, if you are inspired by modern art, and if you love to sew, this book will suit you perfectly. Even if you aren't familiar with any modern art movements or artists but are attracted to interesting designs, want to branch out of your color and standard quilt-block rut, take some design risks, and make unique quilts, then this book will be just what the doctor ordered!

My Project Inspiration
ART AND DESIGN IN THE TWENTIETH CENTURY

As an artist and maker, I am particularly inspired by twentieth-century art and social movements, and by the artists and designers of the era who made new rules while being openly inspired by each other and by their past—the modern art period.

Much of art and quilting history is intertwined with politics and social change. Artists have been, in turn, lauded and despised for their art and their ideals. They have inspired fashion, architecture, textiles, and even car design, while being criticized and very often not receiving recognition in their lifetime.

Even if you are not a student of art, you will undoubtedly have heard of art deco or Bauhaus design, and I am sure you have heard of punk music and pop art and are probably familiar with some midcentury modern furniture design. I'll be deconstructing these movements and also looking at the less familiar but equally exciting movements such as art nouveau, constructivism, Dada, expressionism, and abstract expressionism.

Design and social movements of twentieth-century art inspire all twelve of my quilt designs in this book. I have extracted the aesthetic essence through the use of four design elements: color, text, line, and motif.

How to Use This Book

The designs in this book are accompanied by instructions, so you can re-create them as pictured. However, I encourage you to follow my process of creating a design based on inspiration from your favorite art movement to create a quilt that truly speaks to your style and design sensibility.

Each project includes instructions for how to create the pattern, rather than providing one for you to trace, and also includes four different color palette and design alternatives.

Before you get to the projects, though, I will take you through my process of creating a design. At the end of each quilt project, I include notes about how to personalize the quilt through these four design elements—color, line, motif, or text—or by changing the overall quilt or block size. Learning how you can reconfigure a quilt pattern to your own needs and tastes will open up a whole new range of possibilities for you.

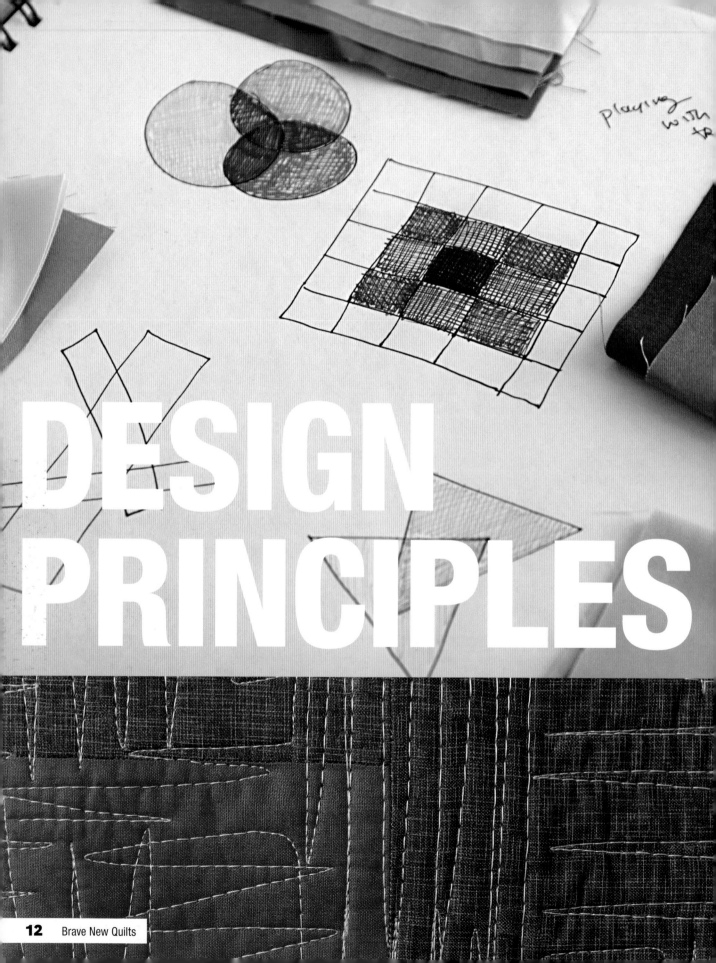

DESIGN PRINCIPLES

When thinking about design, whether it's graphic design, website design, interior design, fabric design, or quilt design, keep in mind several important elements: space, proportion, pattern, texture, line, shape, balance, and color.

Unity in design is the overarching important element. Without unity you can end up with a chaotic, even ugly, design, but you need variety too. Without variety, your design can be boring and stale. Balance is the key—getting the elements in proportion and adding enough points of interest and contrast to create a dynamic, visually exciting design. When all of your design elements seem to really *work*, this is called *gestalt*—a German design term that describes that elusive perfection of when a design seems to come together perfectly. Gestalt is achieved through the control of all the design elements.

Unity in design is the overarching important element.

Space

Empty space is beautiful. It adds an element of calm and elegance to your design. It gives your eye a place to rest. Space, in design terms, is often called negative space or white space. But it doesn't have to be white. Adding space to a quilt design gives the various elements of the quilt a chance to be seen and appreciated—otherwise the design is just too noisy. By controlling space, you are able to create rhythm and relationships.

Seedpod uses "windows," which give the quilt space to breathe.

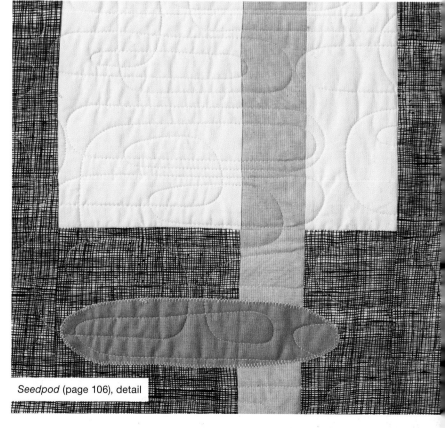

Seedpod (page 106), detail

Proportion

Proportion is the relationship created between different contrasting elements. Contrast, in value and scale, is created by varying the proportion of opposing elements—dark and light or big and small. Correct proportion is the point of harmony between these contrasting elements. Consistently sized elements are not very interesting; it is only when there is a variation that scale suddenly becomes an important tool. This variety in size is a valuable design element and allows you to assign importance, to create relationships between elements, and to move your eye around the design. A harmonious design is when the proportions are right; alternatively, you can deliberately create disharmony between elements with out-of-proportion elements.

The asymmetrical block of triangles in *Peacock Blue* is balanced with appliqué designs on one side and space on the other.

Peacock Blue (page 98)

Pattern and Texture

Textural elements in your design create depth, structure, and a wonderful tactile feature in your quilt. This can be achieved with printed or textured fabrics, with the quilting stitches, or with both. Pattern and texture should complement each other to enhance your design, to communicate a message, and to add subtle detail and interest. Find a balance in these elements; too much pattern or texture can be visually and emotionally overwhelming, and not enough is uninteresting. People respond viscerally to these elements because they evoke emotion and create feelings of harmony.

In *Frothy Nothing*, the quilting adds the textural element.

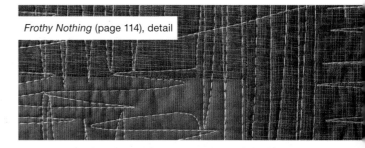

Frothy Nothing (page 114), detail

Line and Shape

Lines connect elements; they lead the eye and create movement, patterns, and relationships. Use line in repetition to lead the eye where you want it to go, to tell a story, or to create an emotional response. The angles of diagonal lines create movement and depth—they are very active and dynamic. Soft, gentle curves are comfortable and relaxing, even sensual; horizontal lines are restful, while vertical lines are lofty and grand. In combination, vertical and horizontal lines are solid and reliable.

Intersections uses a combination of diagonal lines and circular motifs to create a dynamic and active story.

Balance and Symmetry

Balance is that fine line between unity and variety. Equilibrium between your design elements creates balance. In design terms, balance can be achieved in a formal way through symmetry or more informally through asymmetry. Symmetrical balance is achieved when both sides are mirror images of each other. Asymmetrical balance is when both sides are balanced through the use of different elements—for example, several small elements are balanced by one larger element. This type of balance is more difficult to achieve, but it can break monotony and create points of visual interest.

The symmetry in *Sublime Triangle* creates an ordered, balanced design.

Sublime Triangle (page 64)

Color

Color is fundamental to many design decisions and should be thought of at the beginning of the design process, not at the end. Too many colors can be confusing and messy, while the controlled use of color creates a unified and balanced design. Color provokes an emotional response and can provide direction for the design. I'll discuss color in more detail in the next chapter.

Gray Play is an example of controlled color.

Gray Play (page 80)

Intersections (page 40), detail

DESIGN
YOUR OWN

Color

Color for me is largely instinctive. While I do have a good grounding in color theory from my art school years, I don't think about color in a theoretical way when designing a quilt.

However, being familiar with general color theory basics will give you a bit of confidence when deciding on color choices for your quilt or when you are adding to your fabric stash.

THE COLOR WHEEL

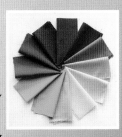

The basic color wheel is a tool made up of twelve colors, divided into primary, secondary, and tertiary hues. It is used for combining and mixing colors harmoniously.

→ Traditional Color Combinations

  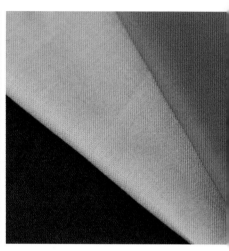

Complementary colors are opposite each other on the color wheel and create a bold and dramatic combination.

Analogous colors are next to each other on the color wheel; this is a serene and peaceful combination.

Triadic colors are evenly spaced around the color wheel and form a vibrant yet harmonious combination.

TYPES OF COLOR

→ Warm and Cool

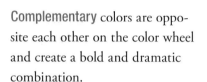

When you hear color discussed in the fashion or design industry, or when you learn to mix paint colors, you often hear colors being referred to as warm or cool. When you look at the color wheel, one side is considered warm—red, orange, and yellow. The other side is cool—green, blue, and violet. Deciding whether a color is warm or cool can be a little confusing and is quite subjective. Certain colors—blue, for example—are normally thought of as cool;

however, blues can be warm if they contain a little red or a little yellow. When looking at tones or shades, you might find it tricky to differentiate between warm and cool colors.

The important thing really is how you use warm and cool colors in your design. Warm colors are generally thought of as vivid and energetic and will advance forward in space, while cool colors are calm and create depth by receding back.

The **split-complementary** color scheme is a variation on the regular complementary color scheme. Choose opposites on the color wheel with an extra adjacent color.

Achromatic color refers to blacks, whites, and grays.

Monochromatic color is the use of one color in various tints, tones, and shades.

→ Tints, Shades, and Tones

The color terms *tint*, *shade*, and *tone* are often used incorrectly. A tint is a color that is lightened by the addition of white. A tone is a color with gray added. And a shade is a color that is darkened by the addition of black. Tints tend to be considered more feminine; tones, sophisticated and neutral; and shades, masculine.

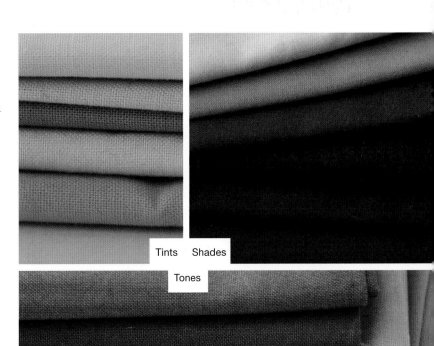

Tints   Shades

Tones

SEASONS AND EMOTIONS

→ Mood

Different colors express different emotions; artists know this and use color to express mood. Dark, somber colors give a very different feeling to a work of art than light, airy colors. You can use color in your quilts to portray feelings too.

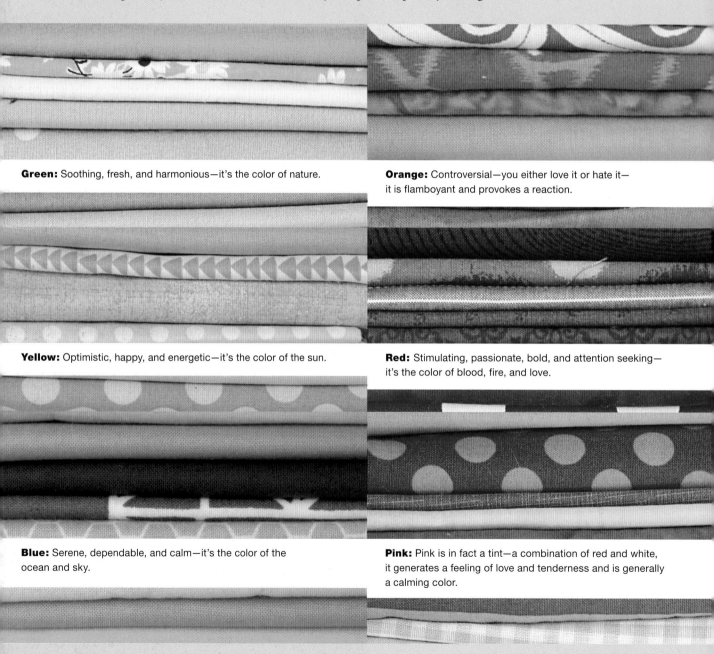

Green: Soothing, fresh, and harmonious—it's the color of nature.

Orange: Controversial—you either love it or hate it— it is flamboyant and provokes a reaction.

Yellow: Optimistic, happy, and energetic—it's the color of the sun.

Red: Stimulating, passionate, bold, and attention seeking— it's the color of blood, fire, and love.

Blue: Serene, dependable, and calm—it's the color of the ocean and sky.

Pink: Pink is in fact a tint—a combination of red and white, it generates a feeling of love and tenderness and is generally a calming color.

Purple: Mystic, calm, rich, and creative—it's a royal color.

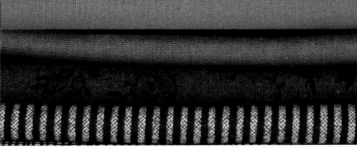

Gray: Neutral and everlasting—it's the color of a cloudy day.

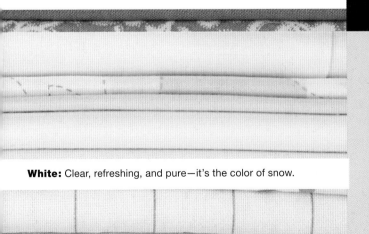

Brown: Earthy, comforting, and wholesome—it's the color of earth—and of chocolate.

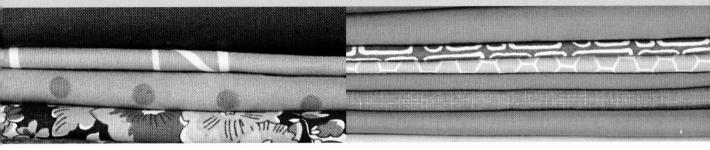

Black: Sophisticated, powerful, and classic—it's the color of night.

White: Clear, refreshing, and pure—it's the color of snow.

Use color in your quilts to portray feelings.

➔ Seasons

Colors also represent the seasons. The warm autumn colors of reddish brown and ocher yellow and the clear, bright spring colors of pink, orange, and green are different from the cool gray tones of winter or the fresh colors of summer. This seasonal change in color is reflected in nature and also has a huge influence on design color trends in the fabric and fashion world. You can see the latest seasonal color trends on the Pantone website (pantone.com).

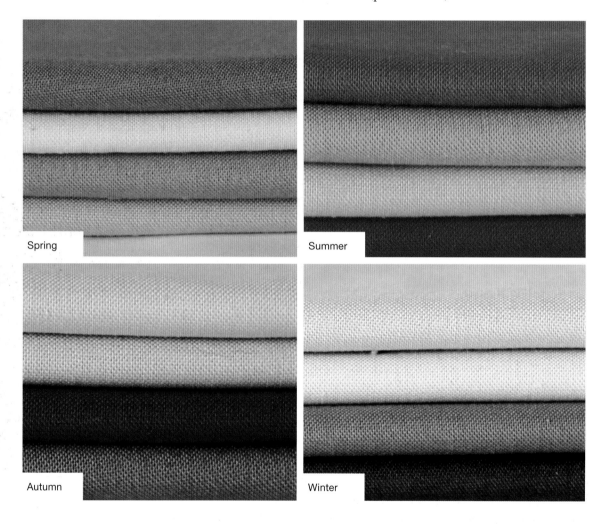

Spring

Summer

Autumn

Winter

COLOR THROUGHOUT HISTORY

Artists and scientists throughout history have been fascinated with the study of color and light and have experimented with color pigments and dyes.

Sir Isaac Newton figured out the first color wheel in 1704. From then on, many artists and scientists have delved into the theory of color. Tobias Mayer, the father of CMYK (cyan, magenta, yellow, and key, or black) color theory, introduced the notion of three "pure" or "primary" colors in 1758. In 1810, Johann Wolfgang von Goethe developed the theory of opposing colors and relationships between colors, and around the same time, scientist Michel-Eugène Chevreul pioneered the concept of color intensity. Today's color wheel is a culmination of all of this previous knowledge as put together by Bauhaus artists in the early twentieth century.

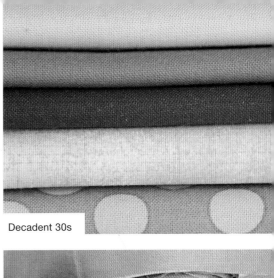

Decadent 30s

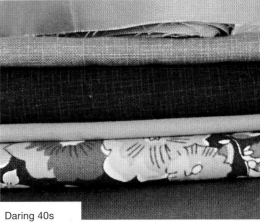

Daring 40s

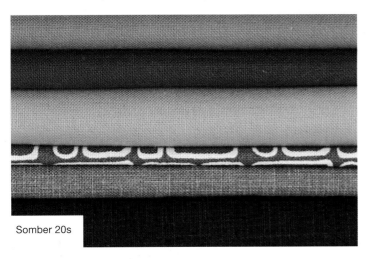

Somber 20s

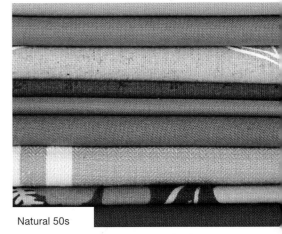

Natural 50s

The use of color throughout history is interesting; the art of each period showcases the feeling and mood of the era. Art nouveau and art deco (1930s–1940s) colors are decadent and carefree, while Russian constructivism (1920s) is sparse in its use of color. Pop art (1960s) is happy and joyful with bright springlike contrasting colors, while midcentury modern (1950s) is full of nature's autumnal hues.

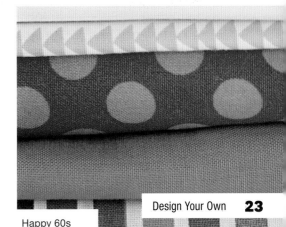

Happy 60s

Fabric

After you have your head wrapped around color—how it makes you feel and how colors relate to each other—you can begin to choose fabrics with purpose.

Fabrics come in such a wide range of choices that it can be both overwhelming and exciting: linens, cottons, voiles, and more, in a range of prints and solids. Fabrics definitely follow seasonal color trends, and you can get an idea about what is trending by taking a look at some of the large quilting-fabric manufacturers.

QUILTING FABRIC

→ Solid-Color Fabric

I am so happy that solid fabrics have come back in style. You can get so many different colors to mix and match with the seasonal prints or to just use by themselves. Happily, you can also buy them in fat-quarter sets. I have a lovely collection of solids in my stash—not nearly enough though!

→ Printed Fabric

Prints

Fabric lines tend to come and go quickly to make way for new ones. My preference when purchasing brand-new fabrics to add to my stash is to buy neutrals, textures, checks, polka dots, plaids, and stripes—these are wonderful, versatile prints to have in your collection. Of course it's fun to buy the latest trendy fabrics, too!

Basics

Neutrals

Textures

Fabric lines come and go.

➜ Organic and Ecofriendly Fabric

Ecofabrics are expensive and not yet widely available. If we want this to change, then we need to support small, local manufacturers who print on organic cotton and linen and artisans who hand print fabrics. These fabrics are wonderful to work with, so do give them a try!

➜ Linen

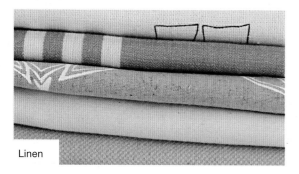

Linen

Yes, you can use linens and linen blends in quilts, and these come in such variety, from dressmaking weight to upholstery weight and everything in between. I always have some natural linen in my collection, and I love those Japanese linen/cotton blend cuties, as well as the wonderful new quilting linens in subtle textures and cross-weaves that have come out recently.

SCRAPS

As you begin to make more quilts and do more sewing, you will end up with a lot of scraps, some tiny little bits and some larger pieces. What should you do with them? It is difficult to discard such pretty things but equally difficult to store them.

➜ Scrap Storage

My scraps are stored—color coded—in large zip-top bags. I have also seen large jars and fabric boxes used for storing scraps; anything you can jam a lot of bits into and easily see what you have is perfectly legitimate.

It is quite useful to have a bin or box near your cutting table that you can throw useful-sized scraps directly into. Then when it begins to over-flow and you have a little spare time, you can sort your scraps by size or color into your containers.

➜ Using Scraps

Using scraps is a fantastic design exercise, too. I like to make color-coded scrappy quilts. Try making a Log Cabin quilt, string quilt, charm-square quilt, or half-square triangle quilt from only scraps. I made oversized Log Cabin blocks from my neutral scraps—beiges, off-whites, light grays, pale greens, with just a hint of darker tones thrown in at random—and I used them for one of my quilt backs (page 147).

Design Tools

→ an inspiration board
→ a visual journal
→ a design wall

These three simple things will help you to collect inspiration, meditate on your ideas, and visualize your designs before you actually begin to sew. There are lots of other tools at your disposal if you have an iPad or tablet, are a little Internet savvy, or can use a computer. You can then access plenty more tools and have a lot of fun with them.

INSPIRATION BOARD

You'll need an inspiration board. Of course, virtual pin boards (such as Pinterest) are great for collecting and sharing ideas, but having a physical inspiration board to look at is the best tool for helping your ideas percolate and flourish.

My inspiration board is not so much a board as a whole wall. I have vintage quilt blocks pinned up next to my kids' photos and sketches, some special postcards, a calendar, artwork from friends, antique crochet doilies, leaves and seedpods, and inspiring words of wisdom. I just pin these directly into the wall with sewing pins. I often change the objects; I rotate new bits that come into my possession and file others away. I like to be surrounded by these little spots of color; they keep me thinking, get my creative juices flowing, and remind me of ideas I want to try one of these days. I also just like the haphazard nature of being surrounded by these ephemeral treasures.

→ Making an Inspiration Board

Your inspiration board can be very simple—a string slung up from one side of the room to the other with your special bits of fabric and postcards pegged onto it.

You could also pin these bits and pieces directly to your wall, or grab some corkboard, cover it with interesting fabric (or just some plain old linen), and pin things onto that. It doesn't matter what form your inspiration board takes, as long as you can see it every day and add little bits to it here and there as you find new treasures.

VISUAL JOURNAL

Next, you are going to need a visual journal or notebook of some sort. It can be a small, plain notebook or a large, fancy journal. I have several of these—and they tend to be a bit messy, with scrawly writing, little sketches here and there, and fabric swatches glued in.

I try to keep each of my projects in a separate journal; this enables me to go back through them for inspiration or just to jog my memory when I'm getting started on a new project. I use my journals for inspirational note-taking, for

rough sketches, for block pattern ideas, as well as to keep track of the practical steps in a project.

You can note interesting color combinations and even special quotes or lyrics you like. Glue in paint and fabric swatches, torn-out magazine images—anything that pertains to your design. If you ever want to revisit that quilt design or show someone how it came to be, or even publish your design, you will have all the information at your fingertips.

DESIGN WALL

To get started designing your own quilts, or even just adjusting a quilt pattern, your path will be greatly enhanced by using a design wall. I know you have heard of these and wondered whether they are worth the effort. I want to assure you that a design wall will be a revelation.

I had read about design walls and even seen pictures of them in use on various favorite quilting blogs, but it wasn't until I saw my quiltmaking neighbor Chris making use of her design wall that I was won over. Her design wall is constantly in use with quilt blocks or embroidery designs. If she doesn't have a quilt in progress, then she uses it as an inspiration board, pinning up fabric or pattern samples to get a feel for her next project.

➜ Making a Design Wall

For a simple design wall, just tack white cotton batting directly onto a wall that receives good light. It doesn't even have to be in your studio or near your sewing table. You can use the hallway or the blank wall in the playroom if you must—just get that design wall up.

You can make a handy, movable design wall by tacking white cotton batting onto a large piece of cork-board, foamcore board, or other large board that is lightweight and stiff. Then, you can move it around where you need it and tuck it away when it's not in use.

ELECTRONIC, INTERNET, AND COMPUTER-BASED DESIGN GADGETS

I love my iPad; really, what did I ever do without it and the Internet? Although not essential, electronic gadgets certainly put a lot of information, inspiration, and tools at your fingertips.

I use the Internet daily for research and inspiration; checking my favorite blogs, Pinterest boards, and email; and of course writing blog posts. I also use quite a few online design tools and websites: color tools (kuler.adobe.com and colourlovers.com), photo-editing tools (pixlr.com), and font sites (dafont.com). Other fun tools include pattern generators (tartanmaker.com and bgpatterns.com) and quilt-block generators (levitated.net/daily/lev9block.html), and more serious work tools like Google Drive and Dropbox (which I use all the time).

But the tools I probably use the most for designing are software programs like Adobe Photoshop, InDesign, and Illustrator—and Electric Quilt (EQ) design software. If you have a few hours here and there to learn these programs, it really is worth it. I sketch designs, scan drawings, fix photos, and design layouts. Designers need to have these tools in their arsenal—but they don't come cheap! Someone who is designing the occasional quilt just for fun is better off going with more accessible tools, such as applications for a tablet or iPad. You name it—there is an app for it: vector-drawing apps, color and mood board apps, photography and sketching apps, and more.

All of these design gadgets are great fun, useful, and time-saving devices. But don't let the lack of these tools distract you from the business of design. Just get out your notepad and pencil and start drawing, and your sewing machine and get sewing!

Design Inspiration

When designing the quilts for this book, I went through a few processes that enabled me to extract what I considered was the essence of the visual aesthetic and the social meaning of each design. Please keep in mind that my findings are completely subjective and based on what I love about these art movements—the colors and lines that speak directly to me. You will certainly find different aspects that appeal to you and inspire your creativity.

HOW TO BEGIN A QUILT DESIGN

→ Research

Research the art movement that interests you. It could be one of the twentieth-century art movements that I have chosen or something different. Or you may prefer instead to research the work of a particular beloved artist. Collect a whole bunch of images, posters, paintings, colors from that era, fabric designs, architectural drawings, paint swatches, vintage fabrics—you name it—anything that is visually appealing to you.

→ Create a Mood Board

Next, create a mood board with your findings. A mood board is slightly different from an inspiration board (page 29). An inspiration board is created when you are looking for general inspiration; a mood board is specific to a particular design. You create a mood board when you have an idea, have drawn some sketches, and have begun to collect fabrics and more images that relate to your design. You could do this digitally, but it is handy to have something on paper that you can immediately reference when required. Then add to it and refer to it during the next step of your process.

Mood board

→ Notice Trends

You'll notice a few patterns and repetitions begin to leap out at you. Make notes of these and create some initial sketches. A particular shape might be used a lot, or a color palette might tug at your heart. I find that separating the use of color, line, text, and motif is a very good place to begin.

→ Begin Sketching

Begin sketching; draw an outline of your quilt and fill it in with some of the lines, shapes, and repetitive patterns you are drawn to. Sketch some quilt blocks, create a repetition, or sketch a whole quilt design. These sketches are still in the early phase of the design process, so make lots of them until you find something that is pleasing.

→ Think about Color

Next you can begin to think about color. How does the artist or era use color? Is the color palette restricted, using only dark tones or bright pastels? For example, Russian constructivism used only two or three colors plus black and white. On the other hand, Bauhaus artists experimented constantly with the interaction of color.

Use an online color palette tool like Kuler.com to create color palettes from an image, or go to a paint store and select paint-chip cards based on your inspiration board. Then, color your sketches using colored markers or paints, or you could use one of those apps or online design tools to create a digital design in color.

Sketches

➔ Audition Fabrics

From your color palettes and inspiration boards, audition fabrics. Solids, near-solids, and small prints feature predominantly in the quilts in this series, putting the focus on color rather than a particular designer fabric. Sort your fabrics into color piles and discard those that don't work, such as fabrics with too much white space or multicolored designs.

Create little piles of fabrics based on your color palettes. This process might take you a while—if you like spending time with your stash, like me, you could be auditioning fabrics all month! You might need to purchase extra fabric, and therefore, you'll need to take your inspiration board and color palettes to the quilt store. This is when a few paint chips come in handy.

Audition fabric

➔ Crunch Time

The time must come when you firm up your design choice: make a decision about block design, repetition, layout, colors, and fabrics. Draw your design using a drawing program, on graph paper, or even directly onto your design wall using masking tape.

CREATE YOUR QUILT PATTERN FROM YOUR CONCEPT SKETCH

→ Quilt Size

Decide on the final size of the quilt based on what you want it for and how much fabric you have. It is very handy to know the standard sizes of mattresses and quilts. The chart shows some common sizes for quilts, but you don't have to stick to these. First, measure your mattress, then add extra on the bottom and sides if you want your quilt to drop down over the side of the bed.

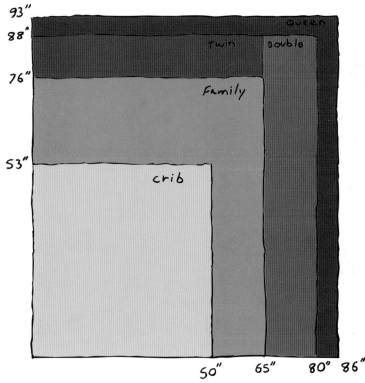

Sizing chart

→ Do the Math

Do some math to work out how big your blocks or sections need to be to get your final quilt size. Some websites (such as vrya.net/quilt) can help you figure out some of these measurements. Or you can work out the measurements on graph paper or in a visual computer program such as Photoshop. Drawing to scale on graph paper will allow you to see the proportions of your design exactly.

→ Sketch on Graph Paper

Sketch your design to scale on graph paper. Draw the quilt blocks and sections. Deconstruct the design and decide how many pieces you will need and what techniques you will use.

→ Create Templates

Create a paper template for your block or motif design. Draw your block on paper at 100% and cut out the pieces. Then, redraw each piece with a ¼" seam allowance around it—a ¼" ruler is handy here. If you are handy with Photoshop, Illustrator, or the iPad application TouchDraw, you can use these instead of paper.

When designing the block size, think about the convenience of being able to use commercially available standard templates and rulers. Also decide what size fabrics you will use—such as fat quarters, scraps, or yardage. Keeping in mind the width and size of the fabric will prevent fabric waste.

Create templates.

→ Test the Template

Now you need to test your template. That's right! Cut out some scrap fabric and piece that block. If you are happy with your design, great! If not, make the adjustments and then piece another sample.

→ Final Fabrics

Choose your fabrics and colors based on instinct, your inspiration board, or your color palette or by consulting a color wheel. Audition your fabrics on your design wall to see how they work together.

Take the Plunge

You are now ready to take the plunge and cut and sew your fabric. You now have the tools and the confidence to put your design in place. Cut up your fabric, sew the blocks, lay them out on your design wall, and piece together your quilt top (see Finishing the Quilt, page 145).

CREATE YOUR QUILT DESIGN IMPROVISATIONAL STYLE

Of course there are other quilt-design methods. You might like to be completely improvisational in your design. A design wall is a must during these processes. I use these methods when creating my quilt backs or if I want to make some scrappy-style free-form quilts just for fun (see Backing, page 146).

→ Jigsaw Method

Sew sample sections of blocks; these can be oddly shaped. Use the fabrics that you have chosen from your color palette, sewing and improvising different designs. Place these on your design wall and piece them together like a jigsaw puzzle. This is a very intuitive way of working and can be a lot of fun. Bring the whole piece together in a cohesive way by choosing common colors, a simple palette, or one neutral background.

→ Big Picture Method

Another instinctive and creative method for designing a quilt is to place fabric strips or pieces directly onto your design wall before sewing anything together; this is especially helpful for an allover quilt design. Cut and arrange your fabrics directly on the design wall. Sew them together and press; then go back to the design wall and add another piece, cut, sew, and press. Continue in this way to create horizontal or vertical sections. Again, you might use one neutral fabric to tie it all together. You'll need to think about this design in terms of the big picture and make sure the overall design is balanced for this to work effectively.

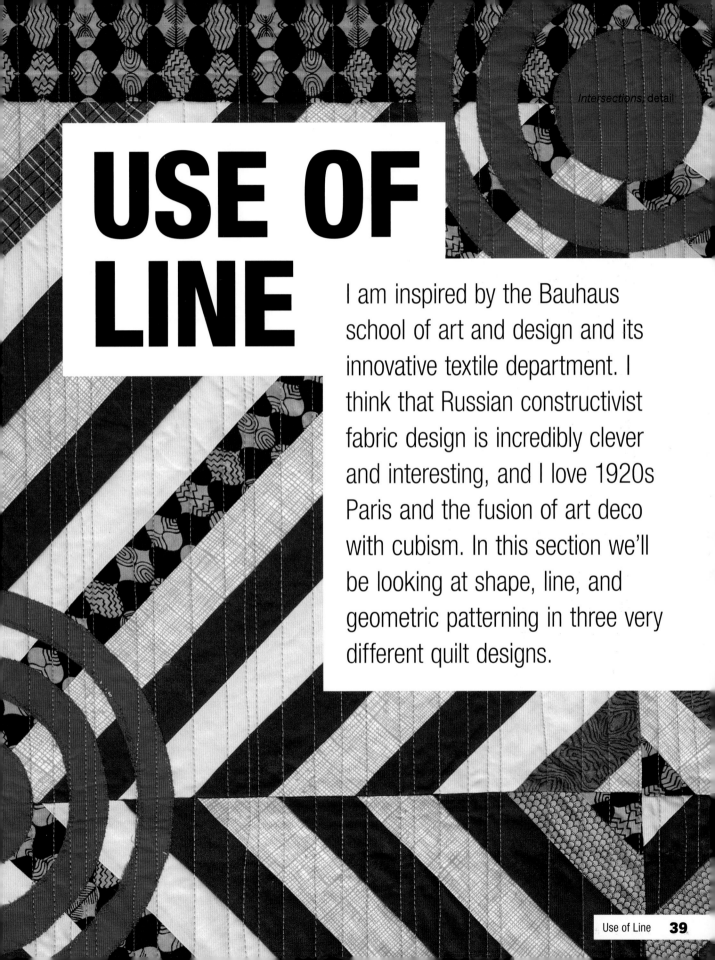

USE OF LINE

I am inspired by the Bauhaus school of art and design and its innovative textile department. I think that Russian constructivist fabric design is incredibly clever and interesting, and I love 1920s Paris and the fusion of art deco with cubism. In this section we'll be looking at shape, line, and geometric patterning in three very different quilt designs.

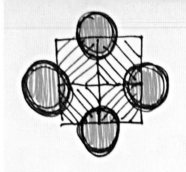

INTERSECTIONS

Constructivism was both an art and a social movement that occurred in Russia during the time between the two world wars. It was an optimistic and pragmatic time, when artists were exploring ideas of freedom and industrial technologies. They incorporated art into their everyday life and took inspiration from all areas: from the avant-garde to folk art. Their artistic endeavors were via public art: theater set design, propaganda posters, fabric, and fashion design.

Even though this movement was situated in Russia, it had a huge influence on artists throughout Europe. Constructivists were exploring printmaking techniques and mass production of fabrics to experiment with color and line. They deliberately chose to keep to a limited color palette to enable them to more fully investigate the relationships between forms. They experimented endlessly with line, scale, and repetition of simple shapes. Their designs were bold and meant to evoke an emotional reaction through the illusory and unsettling qualities of the patterns.

Intersections takes many of these ideas—simple lines and shapes together with a limited palette—to create a dynamic and slightly unsettling design. The patterned border doesn't give any rest, and the bold bull's-eyes intersect the lines.

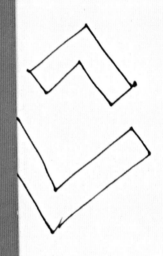

Quilt size: 64½″ × 64½″, couch throw

Difficulty: Medium

Techniques: Paper-pieced strips and machine-appliquéd circles

COLOR PALETTE

Russian constructivists believed in their cause, and part of that was not being wasteful or overly decorative. They preferred to use a pared-back color palette. Gray, black, and white were combined with only a couple of other colors to create their graphically stunning, optical illusionary designs.

In this quilt I have kept the palette very simple, using different tones of gray combined with shocking orange. I love how the orange cuts through the design without taking over.

Materials

Light gray and dark gray scraps and strips at least 1¾″ wide: a range from 4″ to 25″ long in various prints and solids

Bright orange: ⅜ yard

Border: 3 yards of dark gray

Backing: 4 yards

Binding: ½ yard to match your border fabric

Batting: 72″ × 72″

Fusible web: approximately 22″ × 22″

Copy paper or any lightweight paper: 4 squares approximately 18″ × 18″ (You may need to tape smaller sheets of paper together to create larger pieces.)

Cutting

→ 40 dark and 40 light strips 1¾″ wide from the light and dark gray fabrics

→ 2 border strips 16½″ × fabric width*

→ 4 border strips 16½″ × fabric width, sewn into 2 long lengths*

Trim to length later.

PAPER-PIECED BLOCK PATTERNS

1. Accurately draw a 16½″ × 16½″ square on each of the 4 pieces of paper.

2. Draw a diagonal line from corner to corner in pencil. Then draw a line ⅝″ on each side of the center line, and erase the original center line. Continue drawing parallel diagonal lines 1¼″ wide going out from the new center lines to the corners (Figure A).

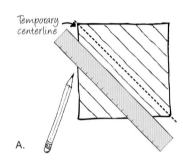

A.

BULL'S-EYE APPLIQUÉ

1. To create your bull's-eye appliqué pieces, trace 4 circles each 10″ in diameter on the fusible web. Roughly cut these out and fuse them onto the wrong side of your orange fabric.

2. Cut out the fabric circles on the marked lines.

3. Draw 4 concentric circles inside the circle: 8″ diameter, 6″ diameter, 4″ diameter, and 2″ diameter (Figure B).

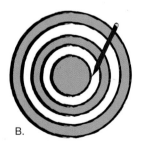

B.

4. Cut out along the inner lines. Keep the outer ring, the center circle, and the middle ring; discard the other 2 rings (or use them for another project).

The patterned border doesn't give any rest.

PAPER-PIECED BLOCKS

1. With the marked side of the paper-piecing pattern facedown, lay a dark strip faceup along one of the center lines. Place a light strip facedown over it, line up the edge, and pin in place, making sure to keep a ¼″ seam allowance extending over the drawn line (Figure C).

2. Turn the paper over and sew on the drawn line. Press the strips open and then line up the next strip of fabric. Continue, alternating light and dark strips until you come to the corners (Figures D–F).

 When foundation piecing over paper, it is useful to use a smaller stitch size than usual to make tearing away the paper easier.

3. Trim the block using a rotary cutter and ruler to measure 16½″ × 16½″ and tear off the backing paper (Figure G).

4. Repeat Steps 1–3 to make the remaining 3 blocks, starting with a light gray strip for two of the blocks.

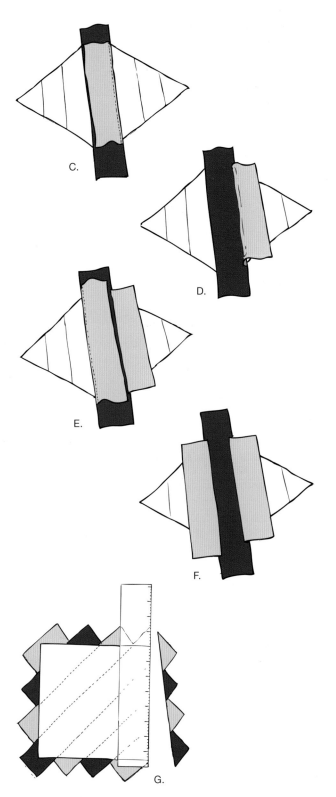

C.

D.

E.

F.

G.

ASSEMBLY

1. Sew 2 blocks with opposite color order together and press. Repeat for the other 2 blocks.

2. Sew the 4 blocks together and press.

3. Measure this center panel from side to side through the center and cut the 2 short border strips to this length.

4. Sew these borders to the top and bottom of the quilt top and press.

5. Measure the quilt top from top to bottom through the center and cut 2 long, pieced border strips to this length.

6. Sew these borders to the sides of the quilt top and press (Figure H).

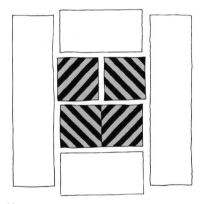

H.

7. Set the appliqué circles in place on the quilt top (Figure I), remove the fusible backing paper, and fuse in place with a hot iron following the manufacturer's instructions.

I.

8. Sew a machine zigzag stitch around the inside and outside edges of the circles.

FINISHING

1. Create a backing and batting 4″ larger than the quilt top on all sides.

I made an improvised design using a mixture of gray fabrics for my backing (see *Intersections* back, page 148).

2. Baste, quilt, and bind your quilt (see Finishing the Quilt, page 145). This quilt was machine quilted with straight lines across the width of the quilt.

Design Your Own

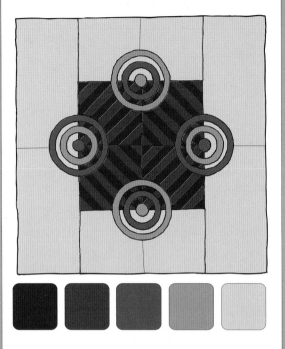

This quilt has optical illusionary qualities that make you almost giddy when you look at it. This is caused by the light and dark diagonal stripes that don't quite meet up, but your eyes expect them to. The patterned border is slightly overwhelming too; on top of that, the bright orange bull's-eyes pulse as you look at them. I love all these aspects; it is incredible that simple line and color can create these disconcerting visual effects.

If you want to keep that unsettling visual effect, make sure the diagonal colors don't meet to make a perfect diamond in the center. Or, if you want to calm down the quilt and make it more ordered and harmonious, then do let those stripes meet up.

Color is a great way to play with the design of course, but I still think that this design requires simplicity in the number of colors used. Keeping the palette to two or three colors lets the design stand on its own (as shown in the examples at left). Try making the center panel shades of orange and/or red and light beiges (or blues or greens), and if you like, try the background in a solid, as this will stabilize the design and push the focus completely on to the center panel.

It is incredible that simple line and color can create these disconcerting visual effects.

WEAVE

The color theorists and textile artists of the Bauhaus school of art and design from the 1920s inspired this woven-look strip quilt. The Bauhaus weaving workshop, headed up by Gunta Stölzl, was very productive and radically modern. Texture, line, shape, and color became the main design elements. These simplified and functional geometric shapes are what the Bauhaus is most known for today—clean lines, precision, and the absence of ornamentation. But also, and perhaps even more importantly, Bauhaus was not only about design; it was about making objects. It revered the handmade as well as the industrially produced, and it managed to reconcile these two opposing forces by making use of technology wherever and however it could, without compromising quality.

Weave is essentially a strip-pieced quilt with a color gradient running through it. The varying widths of the strips, along with the autumnal color palette, create the mood. This gentle gradient quilt has a sharp diagonal line cutting through it, creating tension and interest. These simple lines and sharp diagonals make this quilt visually exciting.

Piecing the strips is the easy part of this quilt. Choosing the colors is the fun bit—a design wall will be a huge help to you here. And slicing the diagonal line and piecing it back together accurately will require precision and concentration—that's the challenging bit!

INTERSECTIONS
gRadient5
oveRLaps

Quilt size: 79″ × 98½″, double-bed quilt

Difficulty: Medium

Techniques: Sewing angled strips and looking at color gradient

COLOR PALETTE

The Bauhaus is perhaps best known for its use of primary colors through its poster and typography design; however, the Bauhaus painting department was central to modern color theory, and their experiments in color influenced modern art and international color theory. The weaving workshop at the Bauhaus used the warp and weft of the fibers to play with color gradients and overlays.

Here, my palette has been inspired by a sunset. The beautiful gradient of color from rich reds and oranges gradually fades to dusky blues and grays. This gradient, though, has a surprise element—the diagonal line, which helps to tell the story of different days merging into one. My daughter has decided that this is her quilt.

Materials

Strips: ⅛- to ⅜-yard strips of 40 different colors (red, orange, yellow, beige, ecru, light brown, darker brown, olive green, light gray, dark gray, and blues) totaling 10 yards of fabric

Border: 1½ yards of ecru

Backing: 6 yards if your fabric is 44″ wide (pieced lengthwise), 7⅜ yards if your fabric is less than 44″ wide (pieced crosswise), or 3⅛ yards if you have backing fabric at least 90″ wide

Binding: ¾ yard

Batting: 87″ × 106″

Planning

Sort through your fabrics and create a plan. I created a gradient that went from rich red through oranges, tan, greens, and grays to blues.

Lay out your fabrics in each hue (include prints and solids), and create your gradients before cutting anything.

Create 6 groupings of fabrics; some fabrics may end up in more than one group. Group 1 is the top section; 2, 3, 4, and 5 are the middle sections; and 6 is the bottom section.

On your design board, mark a rectangle 60″ × 25″ with tape and use a straight ruler to mark the diagonal line between the opposite corners. If you don't have a design board, you can use a large table or a clean floor in the same way (it'll just be a bit more awkward).

Cutting

Only cut enough fabric to create one section at a time.

Sections 1 and 6

➜ Cut 2 strips from each of your chosen fabrics in varying widths from 2″ to 5″ wide and sew them together end to end to create 65″ lengths. (You'll trim these to 60″ later, but this extra leeway will give you room for error.)

Sections 2–5

➜ Cut and arrange the fabric strips for section 2 and then section 3.

Again varying the width of the strips, cut 1 or 2 strips of each of your chosen fabrics for the section you're working on. Place the strips along the taped rectangle, making sure to overhang each strip over the diagonal line by 2″–3″ to allow for trimming and error. It is important that the width of the strips on sections 2 and 3 are in the same order. (You will repeat this process for sections 4 and 5 after sewing sections 2 and 3 together.)

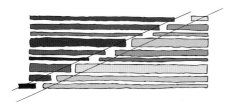

Borders

Cut after the center panel is complete.

➔ Cut 50 pieces 10″ long and 2″–4″ wide from ecru.

➔ Cut 50 pieces 10″ long and of varying widths from your leftover colored strips. (If many of your strips are narrow, you will need to cut more of them.)

PIECING

1. Sew the strips from section 1 together in color order to create a rectangular section 25″ high. Repeat for section 6.

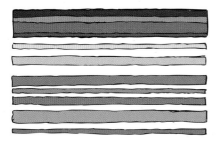

2. Sew the strips from section 2 together to create a triangular section 25″ high; because there is a jagged edge, sew the strips starting from the straight edge.

3. Repeat for section 3. You'll end up with a straight edge and a jagged edge opposite to those in section 2.

4. Pressing the seams open will help with lining up your diagonal seams later. Make sure the sections lie flat.

5. Place section 2 on a flat surface or on your design wall. Use a straight ruler to draw a diagonal line from one corner to the other along the jagged edge. Trim the jagged edge accurately using a rotary cutter and ruler.

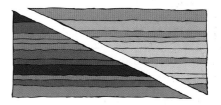

6. Place section 3 on a flat surface. Place section 2 on top, with the cut diagonal line over the jagged line of section 3; be sure the sides, the strips, and the diagonals line up. Use this as a guide to draw a straight diagonal line across the jagged edge of section 3 and then trim along the diagonal line with a rotary cutter and ruler.

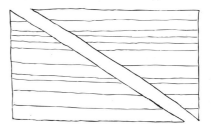

7. Place sections 2 and 3, right sides together, with the diagonal edges lined up (Figure A). Begin pinning at one end and pin on each seamline. When pinning, make sure to leave a ¼″ seam allowance (Figure B).

8. Sew together, making sure to check that the seams are matching as you go. Press.

9. Repeat for sections 4 and 5.

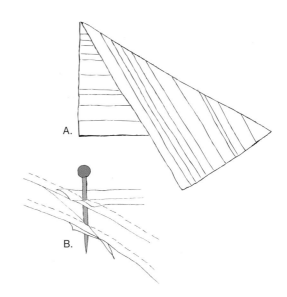

ASSEMBLY

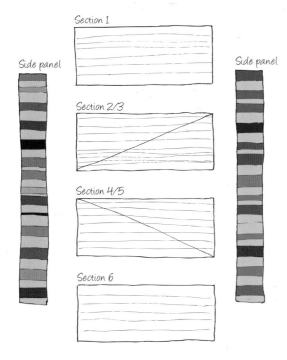

1. Sew the section 2/3 piece and the section 4/5 piece together.

2. Add sections 1 and 6 to the top and bottom to complete the center panel and press.

3. Trim to 60″ wide.

4. See Cutting: Borders (page 51) to cut the leftover colored strips. Piece together the borders, alternating the neutral and colored strips to create 2 borders 10″ wide × 98½″ long. Press and trim.

5. Sew the borders onto the sides of the center panel and press.

FINISHING

1. Create a backing and batting 4″ larger than the quilt top on all sides.

> My backing is an improvised haphazard mix of fabrics chosen from my stash by my daughter. Silvery grays and greens complement the front.

2. Baste, quilt, and bind your quilt (see Finishing the Quilt, page 145). This quilt was machine quilted using a freestyle leaf design. I chose this fanciful design to contrast with the structured lines of the quilt.

The simple lines and sharp diagonals make this quilt visually exciting.

Design Your Own

Using color gradients is a wonderful way to express emotion. Look at sunsets, flowers, and horizon lines to see the way the color graduates in often-unexpected ways. Purple moves through to orange; dark brown becomes bright blue—the colors never fail to surprise.

Play with color gradients in this quilt to create surprising elements and emotional responses, and use imagery of sunsets or horizon lines to inspire your color choices.

The diagonal line cutting across the gradients is a good way to add that element of surprise. Use this wedge section to create harmonies or discord for an emotional response.

Use the alternative design options shown here to inspire you. Be more literal with your color gradients and go with the color wheel or the colors of the rainbow for inspiration. Or, go ombré in your color gradients and fade out a single hue from rich tones through to pastel and white.

Use imagery of sunsets or horizon lines to inspire your color choices.

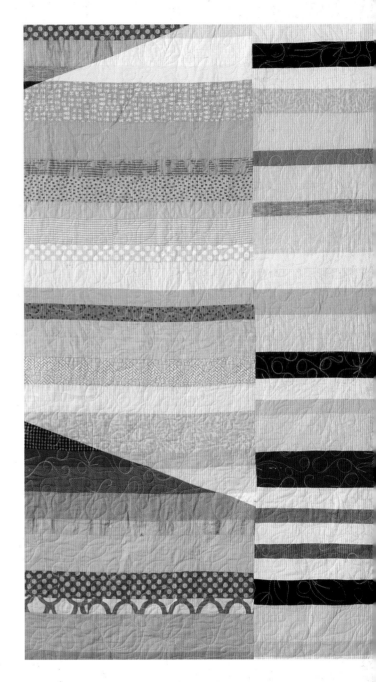

RHYTHM

Rhythm is a combination of what was happening in art and design in France in the 1920s. It is a little bit art deco and a little bit cubist. African masks, Aztec motifs, and modern technology—a real mix of primitive and futuristic—inspired Picasso, the Delaunays, and architect Le Corbusier. Where art deco was streamlined and symmetrical, cubism was dynamic and asymmetric. Cubism was a huge influence on the art deco movement through its love of two-dimensional line and geometric shapes.

These geometric shapes and forms inspired this quilt—the clean, hard angular lines of art deco combined with the distorted, broken two-dimensional shapes of cubism. The variety of the angled lines creates the tension and dynamic movement, while remaining contained keeps them from spilling over into chaos.

Rhythm is a little bit traditional and a little bit not. The blocks are set in a grid design; however, each block has been improvisationally pieced using a method and guide, rather than a pattern and template.

Quilt size: 70½″ × 84½″, twin-size bed quilt

Finished block size: 14″ square

Difficulty: Medium

Techniques: Improvised sewn blocks, pieced together in a grid formation

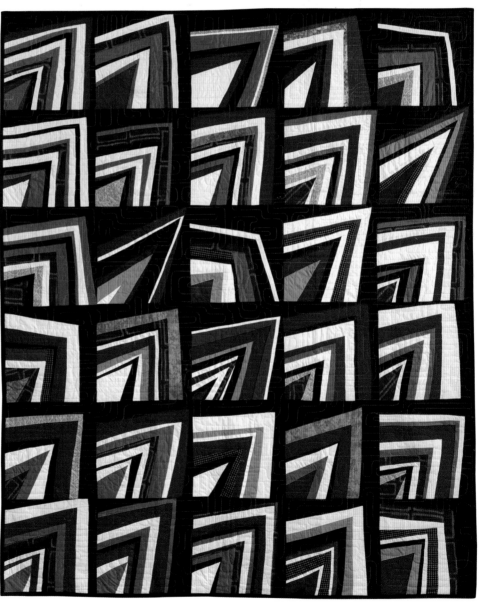

COLOR PALETTE

The art deco period was a time when color was decadent, decorative, and excessive: purple, gold, pinks, and red; but these colors were tempered with cool metallic jade, silver, black, and white. The overall palette was sophisticated and powerful.

I have used a simple four-color palette here: rich purple, tomato red, grassy green, and creamy white. I used one solid-purple fabric to unite the quilt. I was more playful with the greens and reds, mixing up the fabrics and using solids and simple prints in slightly different tones to add movement and a textural element to the quilt.

Materials

Dark purple: 3½ yards

Reds: 1⅔ yards (I used 3 different tomato reds: a solid, a linen, and a batik.)

Green: 1⅔ yards (I used a variety of grassy greens.)

Creamy white: 1⅔ yards

Backing: 5⅓ yards

Binding: ¾ yard to match the background purple

Batting: 79″ × 93″

Butcher paper or copy paper: 15″ × 15″

BLOCK GUIDE

1. Measure and cut a 15″ × 15″ square of butcher paper or copy paper. You might need to tape a couple of pieces of paper together to get this size.

2. Draw a diagonal line from the top right to the bottom left corner. Then, draw anywhere between 6 and 10 angled lines from the center line out to the edges, ending in a point at the top right.

These angled lines are for reference only, and the widths between these lines won't necessarily match the widths of the strips unless you want them to. When using this guide, your fabric will overhang the paper. Don't worry about this; your blocks will be trimmed to 14½″ × 14½″ after piecing.

Use this block guide to help you keep on track of your center point and block size when creating your blocks. It is helpful to keep placing your partially sewn block on the guide as you go to ensure it is not getting out of square.

Cutting

→ Cut 1 wedge-diamond shape for your base piece of the block; use your block guide (page 58) as a general pattern.

If you want to make all the blocks quite similar, you can cut all 30 of these at once in red, green, and white and then make the blocks assembly-line style. If you want to make the quilt more improvisational, then cut the wedges one at a time.

→ Cut a few strips of different widths (2″–4″) from each of your 4 colors, including the purple.

Don't cut the purple background corners until you need them, because these will be different for each block. Cut as you go.

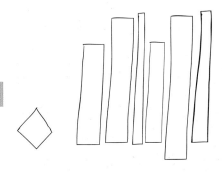

BLOCKS

1. Begin with your wedge piece and sew a strip to one side. Press the strip out. Then sew the same color strip to the other side and press the strip out. Trim the edges straight after adding each pair of strips.

Ensure that your strips of fabric are long enough to cover the corner by allowing a 1″–2″ overhang at the tip. Excess fabric can be trimmed afterward.

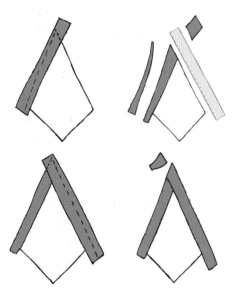

2. Continue adding, pressing, and trimming strips, alternating colors and strip widths as you go, until you have at least 6 pairs of strips or until the top right corner of the piecing is only a couple of inches short of your 15″ square guide. Then, measure and check against your guide for size and squareness.

3. Cut your purple triangle pieces. With the pieced triangle block placed over your paper guide, measure and cut the corner pieces of purple fabric you need to complete your square. Do this by placing a piece of purple fabric underneath the block and over the paper guide and trimming the purple fabric a little larger than needed to the edge. Sew the purple triangle shapes to either side of your angled block and press.

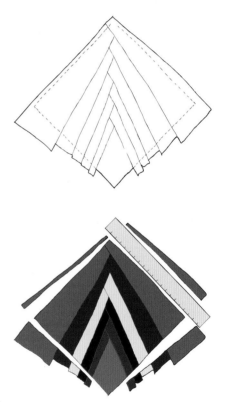

4. Trim the block to 14½″ square.

5. Repeat Steps 1–4 to make 30 blocks.

ASSEMBLY

A.

1. Arrange the blocks in a 5 × 6 grid on a design wall or other flat surface. When you are happy with the arrangement, sew the blocks into rows (Figure A).

2. Press the seams of each row in opposite directions. Then sew the rows together, matching the block seams so they nest when the rows are sewn together.

3. Sew the rows together and press.

FINISHING

1. Create a backing and batting 4″ larger than the quilt top on all sides.

My son chose some favorite black and green fabrics for the backing, seeing he had decided that he quite liked this quilt.

2. Baste, quilt, and bind your quilt (see Finishing the Quilt, page 145). This quilt was machine quilted using a freestyle improvised design.

Design Your Own

Using a variety of angled lines creates a feeling of dynamism and movement in your design. The lines in this quilt, while improvised in part, have a pattern and direction that keeps the design contained. You could make the design even more contained and symmetrical by being less improvisational in your piecing. You could even use your block guide as a paper-piecing pattern if you wanted to be very precise.

You can play with color, line width, shape, and angle in different ways. Because the blocks are improvisationally pieced, you have a greater amount of freedom to take the direction of the line where you want. Begin by cutting your initial diamond wedge in different sizes—longer and thinner, or wider and fatter. You can also trim the strips with a slight flare at the base to create different angles.

As you sew the strips to the sides of your wedge, be sure to include some very thin white strips between the fatter colored strips. These thin white lines will draw your eye to create contrast and direction.

Color is another way to mix this quilt up. I have kept the color palette striking yet simple, using only four strong, bold colors. Simplify and experiment with color by making all the wedges and the outside strips the same color, or make an even number of each. The four alternative color options shown on page 62 are all alternative art deco color palettes.

USE OF COLOR

This section explores some of the color theories that emerged from the Bauhaus school of art and design, abstract expressionism, and color-field artists. The three quilts in this chapter play with color techniques such as transparency, color block, and color gradation, while exploring emotional and expressive uses of color.

SUBLIME TRIANGLE

Sublime Triangle has its design beginnings in the abstract expressionist era in New York during the 1940s. Abstract expressionists created large abstract paintings that were heavily influenced by primitive and children's art and where color was the subject. These paintings were dramatic and liberating and were considered pure—uncluttered by social and historic expectations. They were criticized as anarchic because of their difference.

Jackson Pollock (possibly one of the best-known artists from this movement) and his "action paintings"—both his methodology and the final work—liberated a whole generation of artists from the constraints of accepted art practice. At the same time, Mark Rothko and Kenneth Noland, color-field artists, were experimenting with the spontaneous use of color, giving their art an emotional intensity by emphasizing and using the power of color with simple geometric shapes, abstract lines, and chaotic motion.

Sublime Triangle is a repetition of a simple shape, yet the jarring color combinations are surprising and energetic. My son thought they looked "exotic and very grown-up," while my daughter hated the orange and pink but loved the silver and purple. These colors are supposed to evoke a reaction.

COLOUR

Quilt size: 47½″ × 44″, wall quilt

Finished block size: 23″ × 22″

Difficulty: Easy

Techniques: Triangle blocks sewn Log Cabin style

COLOR PALETTE

Abstract expressionists and color-field artists did not use any particular color palette; their use of color, however, was sensual, symbolic, and emotional.

Sublime Triangle is made with a simple color palette of five fabrics: three solids and two prints. I have chosen the colors deliberately to be forceful, contrasting, and surprising. For the background, I used a gold, followed by a tribal and exotic orange print, a hot pink, a shimmery silver gray that enables the eye to rest momentarily, and last, a solid rich purple to draw the eye inward.

Materials

Purple solid: ¼ yard

Gray print: ⅜ yard

Hot pink solid: ½ yard

Orange print: ¾ yard

Gold solid: 1½ yards

Backing: 3 yards

Binding: ½ yard to match your background

Batting: 56″ × 52″

Copy paper or other stiff paper: 8″ × 8″ piece for template

Cutting

- 4 purple triangles using the triangle pattern on page 157
- 8 gray strips 3″ × 14½″
- 8 pink strips 3″ × 20½″
- 8 orange strips 3″ × 27½″
- 8 gold right triangles: Cut 4 rectangles, each 24″ × 13″; cut 2 of them diagonally from top left to bottom right and the other 2 diagonally from bottom left to top right.

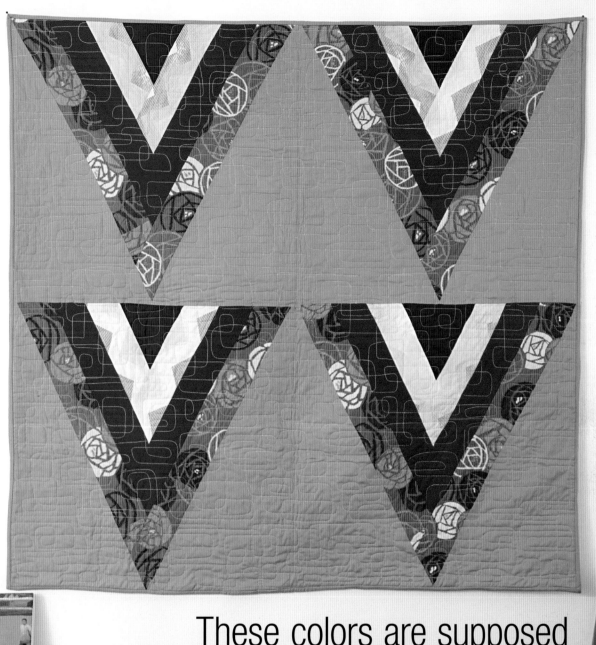

These colors are supposed
to evoke a reaction.

BLOCK PATTERN

Draw a pattern for your triangle base block: 5½" base × 5½" height, and then add a ¼" seam allowance all around. Or, use the triangle pattern provided on page 157.

PIECING

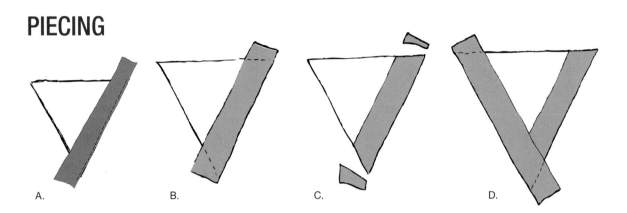

A.   B.   C.   D.

1. Sew the first gray strip to the right side of the purple triangle, leaving a couple inches of extra length at both ends, which will be trimmed after pressing (Figure A). Press seams out as you go.

2. Line up a ruler with the sides of the triangle and trim to the triangle tip (Figures B and C).

3. Take the second gray strip and sew it to the left side of the purple triangle, all the way to the end of the gray strip, leaving at least an inch of overhang at the base and a couple inches of overhang at the tip. Press. Line up your ruler and trim (Figure D).

4. Repeat Step 3 with the pink strips and then with the orange strips.

5. Repeat Steps 1–4 to create the remaining 3 triangle blocks.

6. Sew gold triangles onto two sides of the pieced triangle to create a rectangle shape. Press and trim to measure 24″ wide × 22½″ tall. Repeat to make a total of 4 blocks.

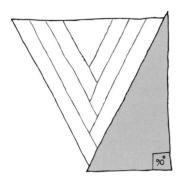

ASSEMBLY

Assembly is easy. Sew the blocks together first in pairs; then sew the pairs together. Press and square up.

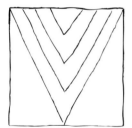 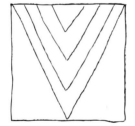

FINISHING

1. Create a backing and batting 4″ larger than the quilt top on all sides.

> For the backing, I chose a vintage print with gold and browns and greens and added some more of that gold solid to create a simple improvised backing.

2. Baste, quilt, and bind your quilt (see Finishing the Quilt, page 145). This quilt was machine quilted using a freestyle improvised design.

Design Your Own

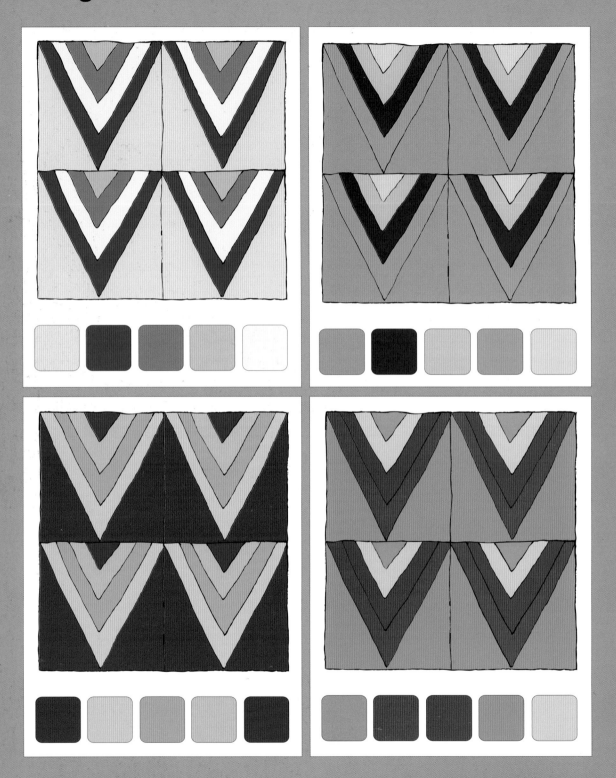

This simple and stylish quilt has many exciting variations to play with. Make the quilt bigger by simply adding more blocks. You could also turn the triangles in opposite directions for an interesting and chaotic variation on this quilt. Or, face the blocks end to end to create kaleidoscope-esque patterns.

I have created four different and surprising color palettes here to inspire you. When the darker colors are in the top triangle and in the background, it creates harmony; when the bolder colors are next to each other, it gives zing to the final design.

This simple and stylish quilt has many exciting variations to play with.

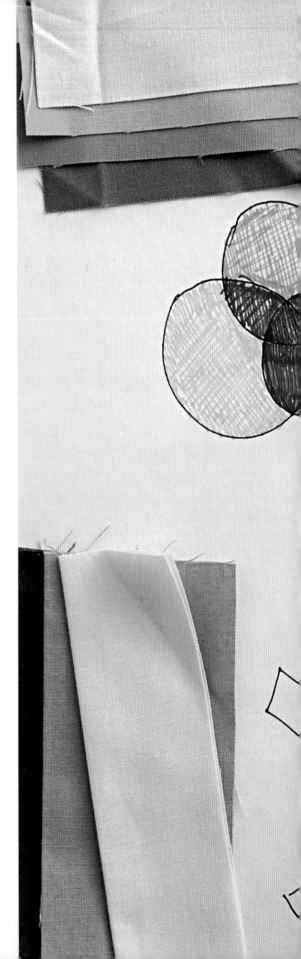

CLEAR CUT

Paul Klee, Johannes Itten, and Josef Albers were extremely influential and advanced in their ideas of color theory, and they all taught at the Bauhaus during its heyday. One of the areas of color that they experimented with relentlessly was the idea of color transparencies and overlays and the illusions that are created by this interaction of color.

Albers used pieces of colored paper rather than paints for his teaching to maintain color precision; he liked being able to repeat the experiment quickly and accurately. In this quilt I conduct my own color experiments, using fabric instead of paper to create a color transparency illusion.

This color illusion and mixture of colors happen mostly in our imagination. For *Clear Cut*, imagine the fabric pieces as translucent plastic sheets, overlying each other, and decide whether the result is believable—it doesn't have to be literal. Some colors work better than others. I have found that the hues need to be clear (tints rather than shades or tones) and in relatively even steps.

Playing with transparency

Quilt size: 86″ × 86″, double-bed quilt

Finished block size: 22½″ square

Difficulty: Medium

Techniques: 15-patch blocks sewn together in a grid formation and color transparency illusion exercise

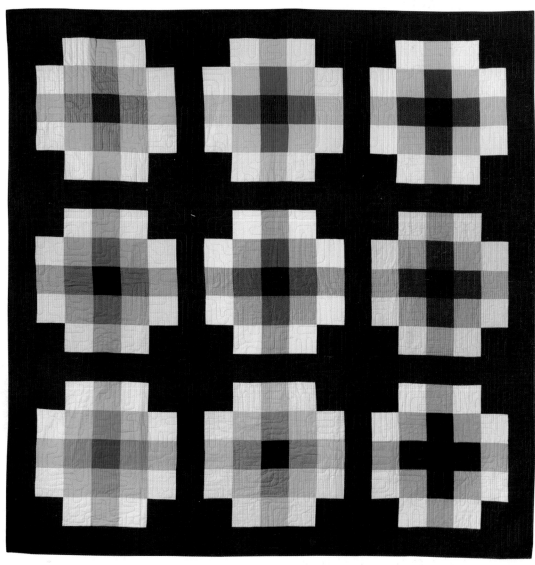

Materials

Hues: 6″ × width of fabric of 36 different hues

Dark gray: 3½ yards

Backing: 7¾ yards or 2⅝ yards of a backing at least 92″ wide

Binding: ¾ yard to match your background

Batting: 92″ × 92″

Cutting

First, cut the long border and sashing pieces along the length of your dark gray fabric as follows:

→ 2 border strips 5″ × 88″*

→ 2 border strips 5″ × 78″*

→ 2 sashing strips 5″ × 78″*

→ 6 sashing strips 5″ × 23″

* Trim to length later.

TRANSPARENCY EXERCISE

This color transparency illusion is caused by the gradation of related colors. Doing this exercise with gray is a good place to start, as you remove the confusion that sometimes comes from working with color. Take a dark gray and step it down to white through four different tints. When you have mastered this simple exercise, you can begin to experiment with other hues. I had a huge amount of fun with this—sorting through my solids and dividing them into color groups, then sorting the groups into sets of four color gradients. Sort from darkest to lightest, keeping the hues clear and pure to get the greatest illusion.

Divide the 36 fabric strips into 9 hues, and then divide these 9 hues further into sets of 4 tints running from very dark, medium dark, and medium light to the lightest.

For each block, cut:

→ 1 square 5″ × 5″ of dark—for the center square

→ 4 squares 5″ × 5″ of medium dark

→ 8 squares 5″ × 5″ of medium light

→ 8 squares 5″ × 5″ of light

→ 4 squares 5″ × 5″ of gray

Put these aside in groups.

The hues need to be clear and in relatively even steps.

PIECING

1. Take the set of fabrics for your first block and arrange it on your table (Figure A).

2. Sew the squares into rows, arrange them again, and press the seams in adjoining rows in opposite directions so they will "nest." Then sew the rows together (Figure B). Press the seams in one direction.

3. Repeat Steps 1 and 2 for the rest of your blocks.

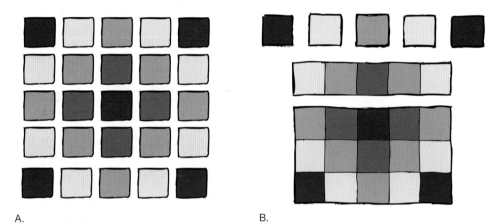

A.

B.

ASSEMBLY

1. Sew the blocks into rows with a piece of sashing between them (Figure A). Press.

2. Sew the rows together with a long piece of sashing between each row. Press.

3. Measure the quilt top from top to bottom through the center and cut 2 border strips this length from the shorter border strips.

4. Sew the borders from Step 3 to the sides of the quilt top and press (Figure B).

5. Measure from side to side through the center and cut 2 borders to this length from the longer strips.

6. Sew the borders from Step 5 to the top and bottom of the quilt top and press.

FINISHING

1. Create a backing and batting 4″ larger than the quilt top on all sides.

The backing (shown on page 149) was a really fun improvised design that I made using my Big Picture Method (page 38) and leftover solid fabrics from my stash.

2. Baste, quilt, and bind your quilt (see Finishing the Quilt, page 145). This quilt was machine quilted using a freestyle improvised design.

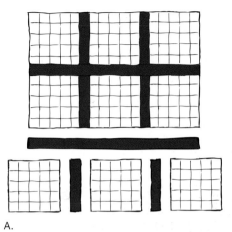

A.

B.

Design Your Own

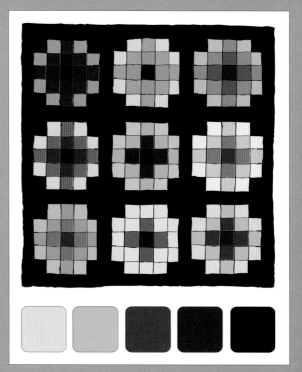

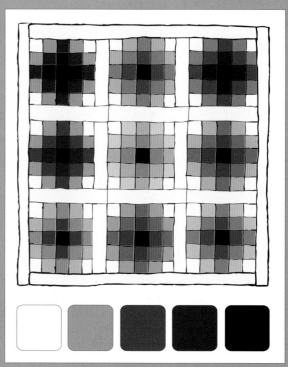

This quilt is seriously fun and easy to make. The biggest challenge is getting those color tints just right to be able to complete the transparency illusion. This is where you will be able to experiment in making this quilt your own: when choosing colors, think of it as four degrees of separation. Paint chips from your hardware store are a great way to get some color inspiration and guidance for these blocks.

Instead of using only solid fabrics, try including some subtle patterned fabrics—tone-on-tone patterns that read as solids from afar would work well. And if you feel that you are just getting the hang of this transparency thing and are getting a bit addicted, why not make more!

You could make all the blocks one single color. Why not change the background fabric too— white or black is a good choice. A solid black background would give this quilt a stained-glass illusion, and a white background would give it an art gallery feeling.

You don't have to stick to logical or realistic color gradations—try some surprising color combinations if you dare!

GRAY PLAY

Artists and color theorists Johannes Itten and Josef Albers are considered to be the fathers of contemporary color theory. Their ideas and written works, originating during their time at the Bauhaus in the 1920s, are still taught in art and design practice today.

Itten was a firm believer in education through play, and his students were encouraged to play and experiment with color contrasts and relationships. He especially loved exercises using tones of gray. Meanwhile, Albers's forays into color theory were disciplined and logical; his long-lasting *Homage to the Square* was a series of hundreds of paintings of nested squares in different color combinations.

Gray Play is an homage to these great color theorists. Using a standard gray square as a base, I have played with the soft tones of gray, exploring the subtlety of color. *Gray Play* is an uncomplicated and even traditional quilt, made of a simple square-in-a-square block in alternating pairs of colors. A medium gray acts as the base or background color with which all other colors are compared.

simple shapes
overlay

Quilt size: 69½" × 69½", family quilt

- -

Finished block: 13½" square

- -

Difficulty: Easy

- - - - - - - - - - -

Techniques: Nine-patch sewn blocks pieced together
in a grid formation with sashing and a border

COLOR PALETTE

Choose a base gray as your starting color. The gray I have chosen is slightly warm; against pink it seems almost like chocolate. I like that the gray seems to change depending upon what it is next to. Because gray is the primary color, the quilt's focus is on the tone of the gray, which helps the subtleties to sing. No two grays are the same; they are pushed to red, to green, to blue—warmer or cooler depending on the light, the relationships with nearby colors, and the color mixing.

As well as the main gray, I have chosen eight other soft gray tones, which work not only as a masculine quilt but equally as a crib quilt or a modern couch throw. Be playful when choosing your colors: pile them up, mix them up, lay them down on top of your gray, swap them out, and swap new ones in.

Materials

Soft gray: 8 fat quarters of different soft-gray-toned solids

Dark gray: 3 yards

Light gray: ½ yard

Backing: 4½ yards

Binding: ⅝ yard to match your background gray

Batting: 78″ × 78″

Cutting

For the blocks, cut:

→ 24 dark gray squares 5″ × 5″

→ 3 squares 5″ × 5″ each of the other 8 colors (total of 24 squares)

→ 2 strips 5″ × 14″ of each of the 8 colors

→ 16 strips 5″ × 14″ of the dark gray

→ 6 light gray inner border strips 2″ wide × fabric width, sewn into 2 long lengths (Trim to length later.)

→ 8 dark gray outer border strips 6½″ × fabric width, sewn into 4 long lengths (Trim to length later.)

PIECING

1. Begin with a colored 5″ center square and sew a gray 5″ square onto each side and press the seams. Then attach a 14″-long gray strip to the top and bottom of the block, press, trim to 14″ square if needed, and that is the block.

2. Make 7 more of these blocks with gray on the outside and a different-colored center square for each one.

3. Make 8 blocks with a different-colored outside and a gray center.

I have played with the soft tones of gray, exploring the subtlety of color.

ASSEMBLY

1. Sew the blocks into rows, alternating a gray block with a colored block, and alternating the direction of the seams.

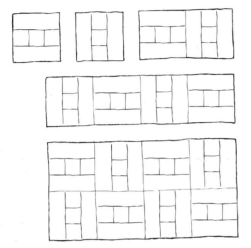

2. Then sew the rows together. Press the center panel.

3. Measure from side to side through the center and cut 2 inner border strips to this length.

4. Sew the borders from Step 3 to the top and bottom of the quilt top and press.

5. Measure the quilt top from top to bottom through the center and cut the 2 remaining inner border strips this length.

6. Sew the borders from Step 5 to the sides of the quilt top and press.

7. Measure from side to side through the center and cut the 2 outer border strips to this length.

8. Sew the borders from Step 7 to the top and bottom of the quilt top and press.

9. Measure the quilt top from top to bottom through the center and cut the 2 remaining outer border strips this length.

10. Sew the borders from Step 9 to the sides of the quilt top and press.

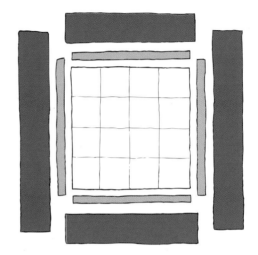

FINISHING

1. Create a backing and batting 4″ larger than the quilt top on all sides.

> For the backing on this quilt, I chose to make a 3 × 3 grid of improvised Log Cabin blocks with neutral scraps (page 147).

2. Baste, quilt, and bind your quilt (see Finishing the Quilt, page 145). This quilt was machine quilted using a freestyle improvised design.

Design Your Own

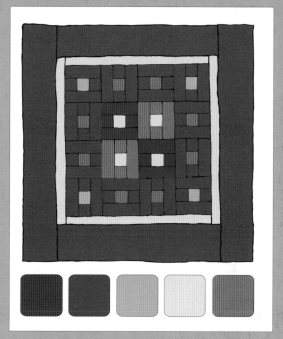

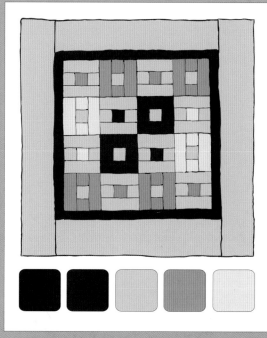

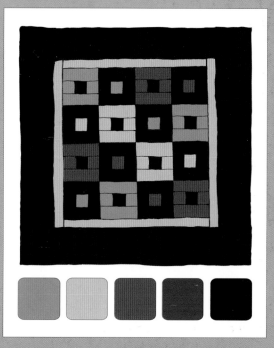

This color-play quilt has so many possibilities, and because the block is so simple, you have time and freedom to experiment with the interaction of color.

An obvious change is to switch the background color to black or white, tan or light gray—or even a non-neutral color like orange or green.

Try some jarring color combinations as well as harmonious ones—you'll be surprised by the feelings that the different color combinations create.

You could try a block in a block in a block, too. Why not three blocks or even four nested squares, as Albers did in his *Homage to the Square* series! And of course you don't have to include the borders—let your design go right up the edge of the quilt for a less-structured design.

Also try changing the size of the inner square. Make it bigger or smaller in relation to the border. Changing the size will change the relationships between the colors, making one more dominant than the others.

Try some jarring color combinations as well as harmonious ones.

USE OF MOTIF

In this section, I take a look at the organic shapes in midcentury modern design, the exotic and curvaceous motifs in art nouveau, and the futuristic elements of art deco. The three projects in this section explore the use of motifs in quilts, bringing a sense of freedom and playfulness to a quilt design.

BRIGHT FUTURE

The art deco movement in Europe and America was full of hope and wonder for the future. It was definitely a reaction to the austerity of World War I, as well as being influenced by the new technological advances in automobile and aircraft design. Speed was exciting; sweeping lines and rounded corners represented that sleek and smooth sense of the industrial and the *moderne.*

Prevalent shapes were chevrons, sunbursts, and zigzags—influenced by Aztec and Egyptian design, but also based on industrial shapes. Patterning was symmetrical, and geometric shapes were repeated. Motifs included stars, airplanes, rockets, and skyscrapers—it was a consumer–machine age.

In *Bright Future* I was inspired by a quilt by Mary Gasperik, which she made after visiting the Century of Progress Exposition (Chicago) in 1934. The block is based on a Nancy Cabot (*Chicago Tribune*) pattern called Star Arcturus, or Rocket Star. Mary Gasperik's quilt, *Star Arcturus—Century of Progress,* is featured on Quiltindex.org.

Quilt size: 36½″ × 36½″, wall quilt

- -

Block size: 12″ square

- - - - - - - - - - - - - - -

Difficulty: Advanced

- - - - - - - - - - - - -

Techniques: Foundation-pieced blocks and paper-pieced stars

Pieced by Julie MacMahon

COLOR PALETTE

The art deco style embraced rich colors, pinks and greens, gold and silver—anything that represented industry and decadence. Black was used as an accent to emphasize the smooth, sleek lines that were prevalent everywhere, from architecture to poster design.

Here, I have used black as more than an accent; it's the ground, while the bright and bold and delicious colors of pink and jade shoot out of the purple and golden stars. I used solid hues of green—a 1930s green and a minty green—and the same with the pink—a salmon pink and a daring pink. The stars are saffron and gold and faded grape and violet purples, in subtle prints.

My friend Julie MacMahon pieced this quilt top together and hand appliquéd the star motif too.

Materials

Black: 1 yard

Pink and green: 1 yard each

Gold and purple: ½ yard each

Backing: 1¼ yards

Binding: ⅜ yard to match your background

Batting: 45″ × 45″

Paper for foundation piecing (such as Carol Doak's Foundation Paper)

Diamond template 3″: for cutting the diamonds (includes a ½″ seam allowance all around) *or* a template cut from cardboard or plastic using directions on page 92

54 diamond papers, 2″ size (You can buy these as a standard size from most quilt stores, or trace the one provided on page 158, for piecing the diamonds.)

Needle and thread or gluestick

Cutting

→ 27 strips 2¼″ × approximately 16″ each of green and pink

→ 9 strips 13″ × 2½″ and 9 strips 11¼″ × 2½″ from black

→ 9 rectangles 12″ × 5½″ from black, cut in half diagonally (18 triangles total)

→ 30 diamonds from gold, cut with a 3″ template

→ 24 diamonds from purple, cut with a 3″ template

TIP Buying reusable diamond papers for your paper piecing is a luxury that is well worth the small extra cost. You'll save yourself lots of time in cutting, and your stars will be accurately shaped. You can also purchase a template for cutting out the fabric.

Motifs included
stars, airplanes,
rockets, and
skyscrapers—
it was a consumer—
machine age.

STAR DIAMOND TEMPLATES

You will use two different-sized templates: a 3″ template for cutting the fabric and a 2″ template for making the papers for piecing (if you choose not to use ready-made papers).

Making Your Own Diamond Template

1. For cutting the fabric: If you don't have a 3″ plastic diamond template, trace the diamond pattern (page 158) onto paper and add a ½″ seam allowance around it. Then retrace this pattern onto stiff plastic or cardstock to create your own cutting template.

2. Whether you use a commercial template or one you've made yourself, draw around the template and then cut out the diamond shapes from your fabric.

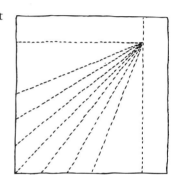

TIP An easy way to trace and cut out the diamonds onto your fabric is to trace the diamond template onto the top corner of your pressed fabric, and then use this as a guide to draw a series of diagonal parallel lines with a ruler and pencil. Then cut out with your rotary cutter and ruler.

Create Your Own Piecing Papers

If you choose not to purchase commercial diamond papers, trace the 2″ diamond pattern onto paper and cut out 54 papers. Accuracy is important here.

Preparing the Paper-Piecing Foundations

1. Cut out 9 foundation papers 12½″ × 12½″. (A 12½″ square ruler is very handy.) Follow the directions in Steps 2–5 to create your foundations.

2. Along the right side, draw a line 1¾″ from the edge of the paper.

3. Along the top edge, draw a line 1¾″ from the edge of the paper.

4. At the intersecting point, draw a diagonal line to the opposite corner.

5. Then draw 3 more diagonal lines radiating out from the point on each side of the center diagonal line; these should be 2″ apart at the outside edges. You now have your foundation-piecing pattern. Make a total of 9 foundations.

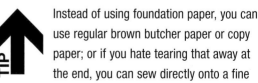

TIP Instead of using foundation paper, you can use regular brown butcher paper or copy paper; or if you hate tearing that away at the end, you can sew directly onto a fine (nonfusible) interfacing or muslin. If you use interfacing, use a walking foot to prevent slippage.

FOUNDATION-PIECED BLOCKS

1. Place the foundation paper on a surface with the drawn lines facedown.

2. On the unmarked top of the foundation paper, place your first colored strip of fabric right side up over the angled line farthest to the right, making sure to overlap your fabric at least the width of the seam allowance. Place the next colored strip of fabric right side down on top and pin in place.

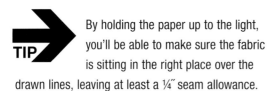

TIP By holding the paper up to the light, you'll be able to make sure the fabric is sitting in the right place over the drawn lines, leaving at least a ¼˝ seam allowance.

3. Turn the paper over, marked side up, and sew directly on the first line through the paper and the fabric.

4. Remove the paper foundation from the sewing machine. Fold the paper out of the way and use a ¼˝ ruler to trim the seam allowance neatly. Then, press open the strips.

5. Repeat Steps 2–4 for the remaining sunburst strips, alternating the colors.

6. Attach the background triangles using the same method and press open.

7. Lastly, add the background strips along the top and side. Press open.

8. Trim the block to measure 12½˝ × 12½˝; then tear off the foundation paper backing.

9. Repeat Steps 1–8 for the remaining 8 blocks.

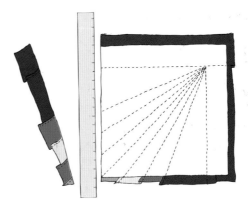

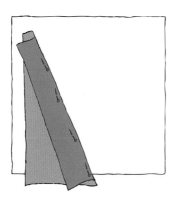

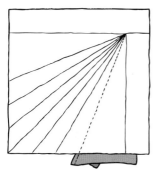

STAR BLOCKS

1. Place the diamond paper template over the wrong side of your cut-out diamond fabric, turn over the seam allowance neatly, and use either a gluestick or a needle and thread to baste the fabric in place around the diamond (Figure A). On the two sharper end points of the diamond, you might try folding in the tip of fabric first, and then the seam allowances, to create a mitered corner. Do this for all the diamonds.

2. Then, sew the diamonds together to make a 6-pointed star: With the paper still inside and with right sides together, whipstitch the diamonds together along one edge; don't stitch through the paper (Figure B). Continue adding diamonds around the edges until you have a star shape (Figure C).

3. Remove the papers and pin the stars onto the corners of your sunburst blocks. Baste them on first with a little basting glue (or pin them). And then either hand sew (if you are in the swing of hand sewing) or use small neat stitches to machine sew them in position (Figure D).

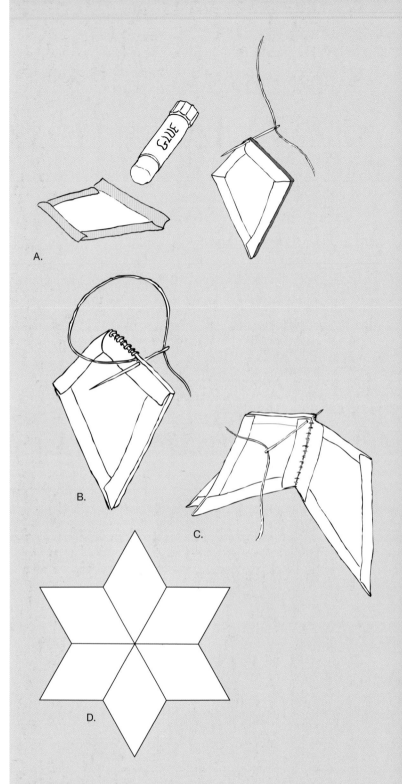

A.

B.

C.

D.

ASSEMBLY

1. Sew the blocks into rows, with all the sun-bursts facing the same direction (Figure A).

2. Sew the rows together.

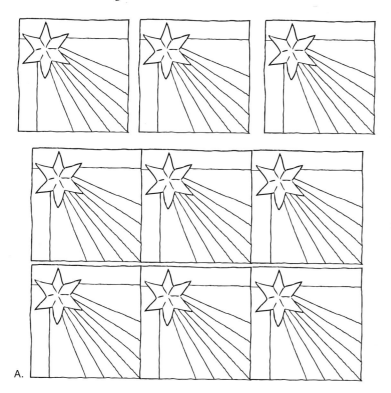

A.

FINISHING

1. Create a backing and batting 4″ larger than the quilt top on all sides.

For the backing on this quilt, I created a simple backing using an elegant print with the same colors as the front.

2. Baste, quilt, and bind your quilt (see Finishing the Quilt, page 145). This quilt was machine quilted using a freestyle improvised design.

Design Your Own

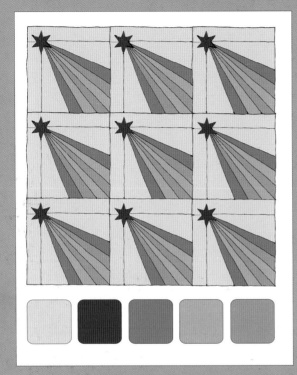

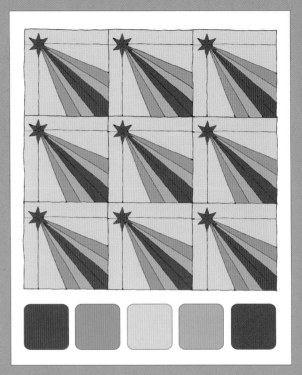

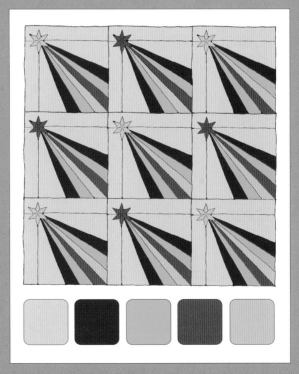

I sort of feel like this design already has such classic perfection that you shouldn't fiddle with it too much. But, well … since I have already gone ahead and played with the original, you may as well do the same.

Adjust the scale of the stars; they can be made much smaller, and extra stars could be added all around too. While you are adjusting the scale of elements, try making the sunbursts wider. Make more repetitions. The quilt I was originally inspired by was a 6 × 5 grid, with the sunburst block alternating with a simpler star block; it also had an intricate scalloped edging and was orange, yellow, and pale blue.

I encourage you to try alternating the sunburst block with a plain block—giving the quilt more breathing space.

Changing the colors, the scale, and the size will allow you to personalize this quilt as you like.

PEACOCK BLUE

Art nouveau (from the early twentieth century) was an artistic reaction to history. *Art nouveau* literally means "new art," and this art movement affected craft, art, and architecture. It was elegant and innovative, and over the top with decorative patterning and asymmetrical curvaceous lines. Gustav Klimt is possibly the most famous artist from this era; his golden paintings of women wrapped in richly patterned fabrics and decorated in swirling designs were a big influence on *Peacock Blue*.

Common art motifs used in this period included exotic and beautiful animals and plants such as the peacock, swan, dragonfly, and lily, as well as intertwining, naturally curvy, asymmetrical forms such as circular shapes, swirls, crescents, and whiplash swishes.

Peacock Blue is made of a richly patterned, off-center panel in colors from this era, and the side panel has a peacock-inspired motif wending its way upward. This asymmetrical quilt is exotic and decorative, but the silvery gray background gives it space to breathe.

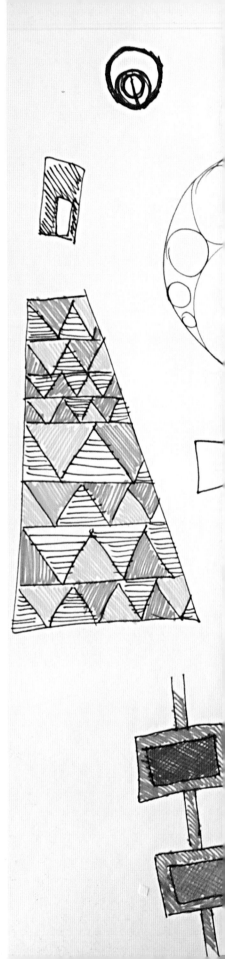

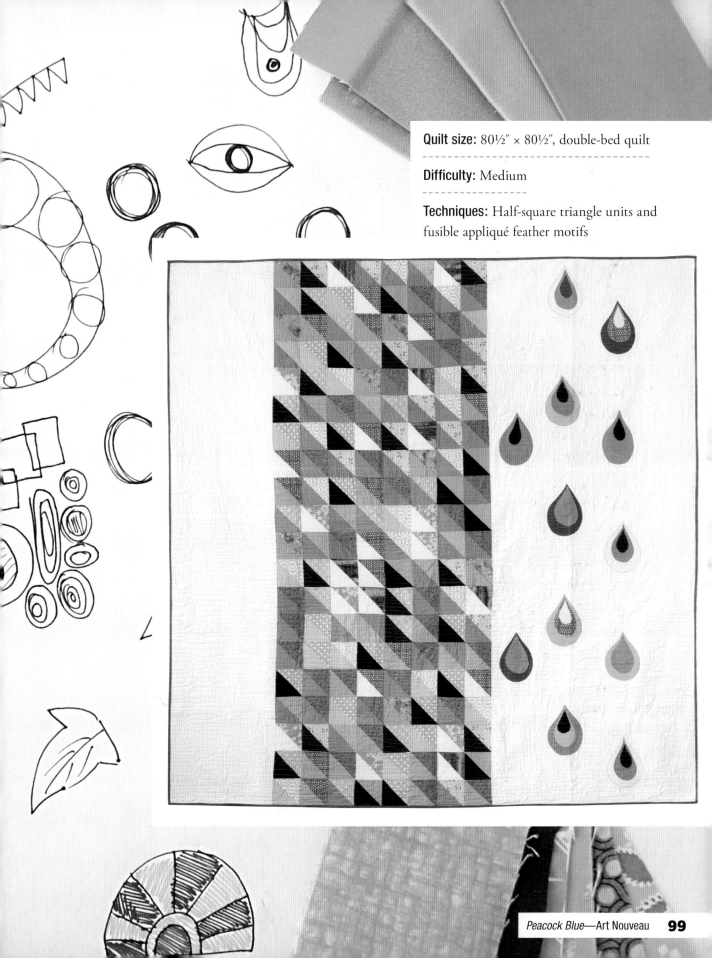

Quilt size: 80½″ × 80½″, double-bed quilt

Difficulty: Medium

Techniques: Half-square triangle units and fusible appliqué feather motifs

Colors in this era were rich and luxurious and exotic. Peacock blues, purples, and greens are synonymous with this era, as are gold and shades of bronze and silver.

For this quilt I took my color palette almost literally from the peacock. The central panel is made of a series of half-square triangles in rich blues, greens, and golds, and the appliqué motifs on the right have picked up a few of these feature fabrics. The background fabric is a silvery gray.

Materials

Gold, turquoise, sea green, and peacock blue: 6–10 different fabrics (3 yards total)

Silver gray: 3½ yards

Backing: 7½ yards, or 2½ yards if using a wide backing at least 90″ wide

Binding: ¾ yard

Batting: 89″ × 89″

Fusible web: approximately 30″ × 40″

Cutting

→ 40 squares 10″ × 10″ from different fabrics for the half-square triangles

→ 10 squares 17″ × 17″ from background fabric

→ 2 pieces 16½″ × fabric width, sewn together and trimmed to make 1 strip 16½″ × 80½″ for the left side of the quilt

FUSIBLE APPLIQUÉ

1. Trace the appliqué patterns onto the fusible web. You'll need to trace 12 each of the small and medium and large patterns on page 158; then roughly cut them out and fuse them onto scraps of leftover colored fabric.

2. Use a small pair of sharp scissors to neatly cut out the pieces.

3. Remove the backing paper from the smallest and the medium-size appliqué shapes (not the large one just yet). Layer the 3 shapes in order of size and fuse together following the manufacturer's instructions.

4. Remove the backing paper from the large appliqués and arrange them on top of the 17″ background squares. Make sure to leave at least ¾″ free around the edge of each square for trimming and seam allowance. Fuse into position.

5. Sew around the outside edge of each appliqué piece to secure it into position.

6. Trim each block to measure 16½″ × 16½″ square.

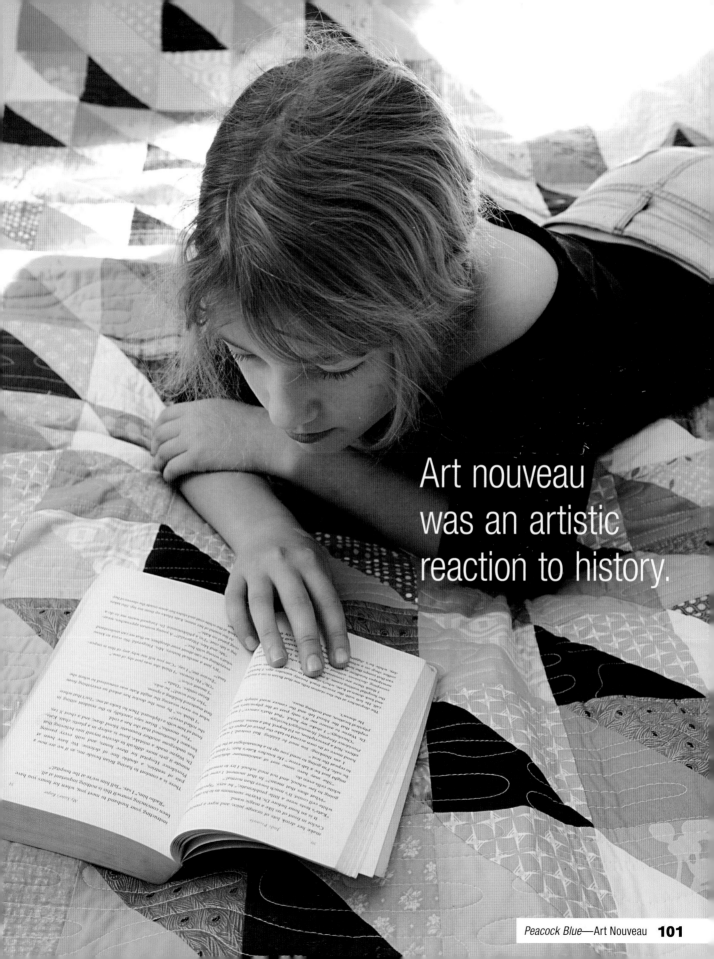

Art nouveau
was an artistic
reaction to history.

HALF-SQUARE TRIANGLE UNITS

1. Place 2 of the 10″ × 10″ squares right sides together (contrasting colors, or one solid and one patterned fabric) and pin (Figure A).

2. Draw 2 diagonal lines from corner to corner (Figure B).

3. Sew a ¼″ seam on each side of these 2 lines (Figure C). Repeat these steps for all 20 pairs.

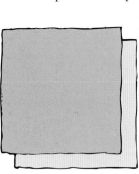

A.

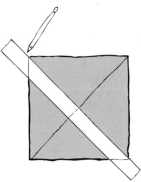

B.

C.

4. Cut a vertical and a horizontal line down the center of each set. Then cut on the drawn diagonal lines. Press each half-square triangle open (Figure D) and trim to 4½″ × 4½″ as necessary.

5. You'll get 8 half-square triangle units 4½″ × 4½″ from each set. Press them flat and square them up, treating the bias edges gently. Make 160 units.

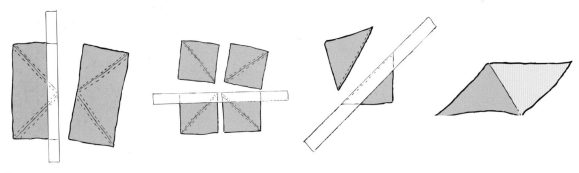

D.

6. Arrange the units in rows of 8; I put all my printed fabrics facing upward. Sew into rows; press the seams going in one direction in each row but alternating directions from one row to the next so that seams will "nest." Then sew the rows together, matching the seams.

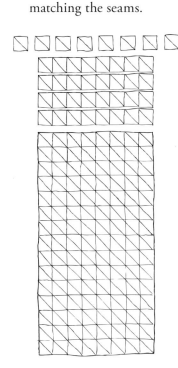

ASSEMBLY

1. Sew the 16½″ × 16½″ appliqué squares together in rows and press. Sew the rows together and press (Figure A).

2. Sew the sections together and press.

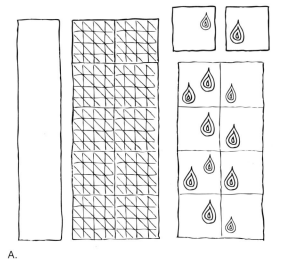

A.

FINISHING

1. Create a backing and batting 4″ larger than the quilt top on all sides.

For the backing on this quilt, I created an off-center panel of crazy scrappy blocks left over from the front, and finished up with soft linen (page 148).

2. Baste, quilt, and bind your quilt (see Finishing the Quilt, page 145). This quilt was machine quilted using a freestyle improvised design.

Design Your Own

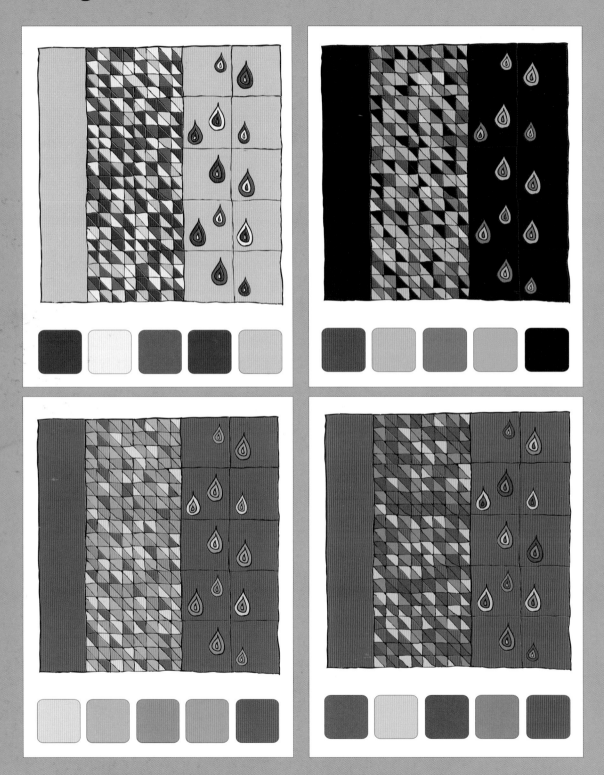

This quilt has two main elements that give it that art nouveau style: color and motif. Try some of these different color palettes—all from the nouveau era. Or, when coming up with your own color palette, think rich gold and bronze; decadent purple, turquoise, and lapis lazuli; and jade green and ruby red—all offset by silvery gray.

Motifs are also a major part of this era. Try an Egyptian-style eye shape or some golden swirls and whiplashes (you can make these from bias tape). You could get really creative with decorative patterning and ornate designs. In fact, this is one of the most creatively expressive parts of this quilt—making the motif you choose fit with your design aesthetic. I love that this era was so rich in design inspiration.

Get really creative with decorative patterning and ornate designs.

Midcentury Modern

SEEDPOD

Midcentury modern was an exciting design movement that made its appearance in the 1950s. From fabric and furniture to architecture and objects, midcentury modern designers took the Bauhaus ideas of simplicity, practicality, and style and further integrated natural colors, shapes, and textures. Hard lines became more organic, and colors softened, too.

Designers such as American couple Charles and Ray Eames and Finnish couple Aino and Alvar Aalto were groundbreaking in their harmonious, practical, and playful designs, which incorporated organic human-friendly shapes, new technologies, and an optimistic attitude.

Seedpod is influenced largely by midcentury textile designs, with organic shapes such as seedpods, leaves, and river stones. *Seedpod* is a harmonious design, with plenty of space; the lines and blocks are broken and softened by organic-shaped motifs and a textured background fabric.

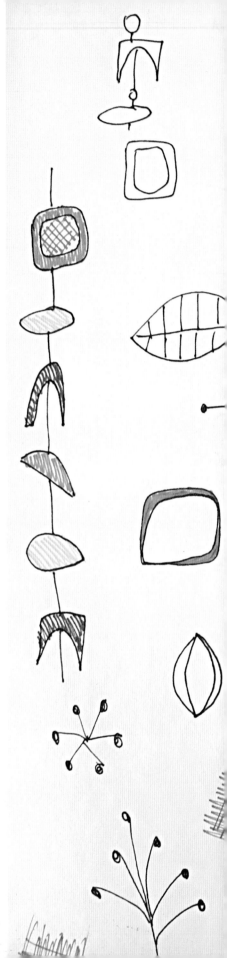

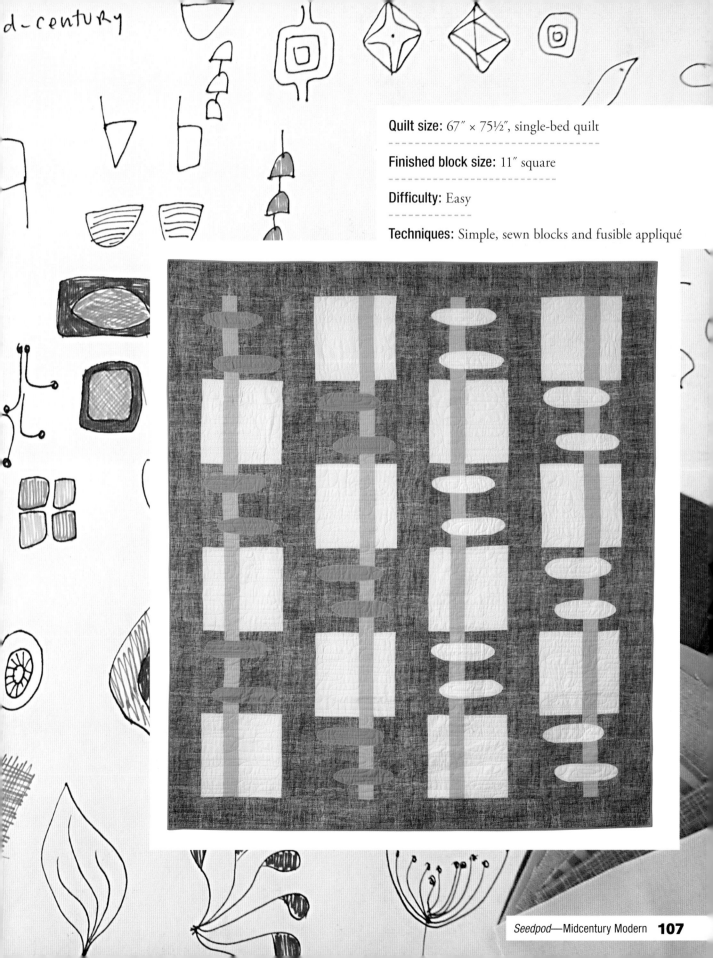

Quilt size: 67″ × 75½″, single-bed quilt

Finished block size: 11″ square

Difficulty: Easy

Techniques: Simple, sewn blocks and fusible appliqué

COLOR PALETTE

The midcentury modern color palette was taken from the natural world, with plenty of brown and ocher tones, sage green, brick red, charcoal, soft pinks, soft grays, and soft blues.

I have used only five fabrics in this quilt. The crosshatch sketchy black-and-white background fabric gives the impression of textured gray from far away and is combined with natural linen "vines," soft blue "windows," and simple white and earthy golden bean-pod-shaped motifs.

Materials

White and gold: ⅜ yard each for the appliqué motifs

Light blue: 1¼ yards

Natural linen: ⅔ yard

Background: 3⅛ yards

Backing: 4¾ yards

Binding: ¾ yard to match your background

Batting: 75″ × 84″

Fusible web: approximately 20″ × 40″ (*optional; see tip below*)

 TIP Use a few dabs of appliqué glue or pins, rather than fusible web, on the appliqué motifs, especially if you don't intend to quilt over the motifs and want them to puff up a little to give them a slight dimensional shape and definition.

Cutting

Light blue
→ 4 strips 3½″ × fabric width
→ 4 strips 6″ × fabric width

Natural linen
→ 8 strips 2½″ × fabric width

Background
→ 4 strips 3½″ × fabric width
→ 4 strips 6½″ × fabric width
→ 9 vertical sashing and border strips 5″ × fabric width, sewn into 1 long length*
→ 4 border strips 5″ × fabric width, sewn into 2 long strips for the top and bottom borders*

* Trim to length later.

Seedpod is a harmonious design, with plenty of space.

SEEDPOD APPLIQUÉ

1. Draw a rectangle approximately 3″ × 10″. Round off the corners with organic imperfect lines. You could also make up your own seedpod designs. Some ideas can be found in the mood board pictured on pages 106 and 107.

2. Trace 24 of these shapes onto fusible web.

3. Fuse 12 of them onto the back of the white fabric and 12 onto gold fabric.

4. Cut out all of the shapes on the marked lines.

PIECING AND FUSING

1. Sew a linen strip between a 3½″-wide and a 6½″-wide blue strip and press. This strip set should measure 11½″ wide. Repeat to make 4 sets.

2. Repeat Step 1 using the remaining linen strips together with the 3½″-wide and 6½″-wide background strips.

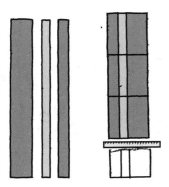

3. Trim the sets from Steps 1 and 2 into 11½″ × 11½″ blocks; you will get 3 blocks from each set. You will have 12 linen/blue blocks and 12 linen/background blocks. Press the blocks nice and flat.

4. Remove the paper backing from the appliqué motifs. Position the motifs on the background block, overlapping the linen strip. Fuse to the pieced background fabric, following the manufacturer's instructions.

5. Sew around the motifs using a zigzag (or other similar stitch) to secure in place. Press the motifs down flat.

ASSEMBLY

1. Sew the blocks in vertical rows, alternating blue and background blocks, and press.

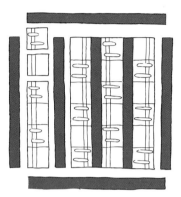

2. Measure the length of your rows and find the average length. Trim 5 vertical sashing/border strips to this length.

3. Sew 3 of the sashing/border strips between the pieced strips and 1 on each side of the quilt top for the side borders.

4. Measure the quilt top from side to side through the center and trim the remaining 2 border strips to this length.

5. Sew the top and bottom border strips to the quilt top and press the whole quilt top.

FINISHING

1. Create a backing and batting 4″ larger than the quilt top on all sides.

For the backing on this quilt, I used a beautiful piece of vintage bark cloth in similar colors with dark charcoal linen.

2. Baste, quilt, and bind your quilt (see Finishing the Quilt, page 145). This quilt was machine quilted using a freestyle improvised design.

Design Your Own

One of the best parts of designing this quilt, for me, was sketching the seedpod designs, and I encourage you to do the same. Of course, you can use the same bean-pod shape I did, but if you want to make this quilt your own, collect some seedpods from around where you live and spend a little time sketching their outlines, very simply. You don't need to be an artist for this task—and it's fun, too.

Look at my mood board (page 106 and 107) for some alternative seedpod shapes you can use for inspiration. Mixing up and using lots of different motifs within the quilt could be interesting, too.

And of course you can change up the color palette. I like the idea of this quilt being gray, yellow, black, and blue or brick red, mushroom pink, sage green, and soft gray. I have included four different color palettes from this era (page 112) for you to consider.

Collect some seedpods and spend a little time sketching.

Design Your Own

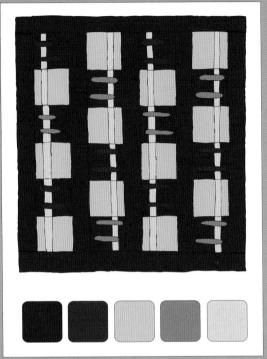

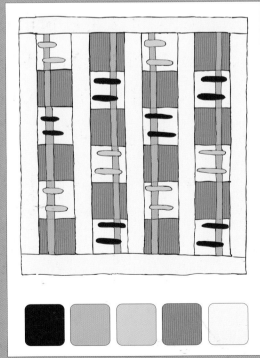

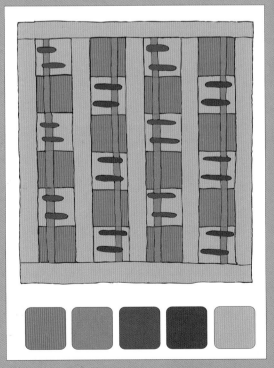

USE OF TEXT

This is perhaps the most challenging section, in terms of pushing the boundaries of your comfort zone with technique and aesthetics, but maybe the most exciting, too. I'll be taking a look at three art movements that use words, text, and typography as a major part of their expression: the 1920s "anti-art" movement, Dada, with its nonsense poetry; the punk music scene, where lyrics were central; and pop art, with a seemingly empty ethos that was surprisingly vocal.

FROTHY NOTHING

Dada has to be one of my very favorite art movements of the twentieth century—although it is not so much an art movement as a short-lived phenomenon. It was a protest against war and consumerism; it was anarchic but organized, cynical but clever, incorporating abstract, collage, and found art as well as theater and poetry. It is perhaps the random poetry and performance aspects, as well as the many manifestos, that excite me the most.

The Dada movement began in Zurich in 1916 and captured the imagination of artists from all over Europe and the United States. While Marcel Duchamp made Dada infamous through his found art assemblage—his "ready-mades"—Hugo Ball and Tristan Tzara were writing their Dada manifestos. Ball explains the Dada movement as being a "piece of tomfoolery from the void" and reality as a "frothy nothing," while Tzara, at the end of his manifesto, says that Dada is "without pretension, as life should be."

The text in *Frothy Nothing* comes from the quote from Hugo Ball. I love the Dada nonsense poetry and play with words, and because they loved words so much, Dadaists explored typography in their poster art. I used an old-fashioned letterpress font, similar to that of the poster art during this era.

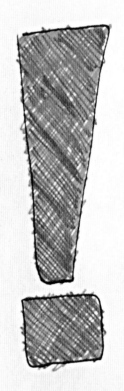

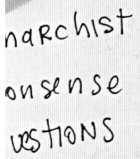

narchist
onsense
uestions

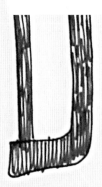

Quilt size: 36″ × 49″, wall quilt

Difficulty: Easy

Techniques: Simple, pieced whole quilt and machine-stitched appliqué lettering

COLOR PALETTE

Because the Dada artists were involved mainly in performance and spoken art, they published posters, typographic works, and pamphlets and made collages and found works of art. They used simple colors, nothing fancy or decorative—it was all very pragmatic.

In this quilt, I have tried to replicate the clever typographic poster design from that era, using natural, faded, printed inks and dyed papers and a simple three-color palette. The red is not really red but a faded pink-red, and the gray is a lightly textured quilting linen.

Materials

Background: 1½ yards

Faded red: ⅝ yard

Blue: ⅜ yard

Backing: 2½ yards

Binding: ½ yard to match your background

Batting: 44″ × 57″

Fusible web: approximately 12″ × 40″

Cutting

Background

➜ 2 strips 10″ × 40″ for side borders

➜ 2 strips 5¼″ × 32″

➜ 1 strip 2½″ × 17″

➜ 2 strips 5″ × 36″ for top and bottom borders

Red

➜ 1 rectangle 10½″ × 17″

➜ 1 rectangle 17″ × 28″

Using the 17″ × 28″ red rectangle, measure and then mark 5″ in from each top corner on the 17″ side. Draw a straight line from these marks to the bottom corners. Cut along this line. Discard the triangle pieces.

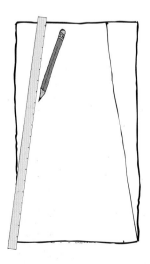

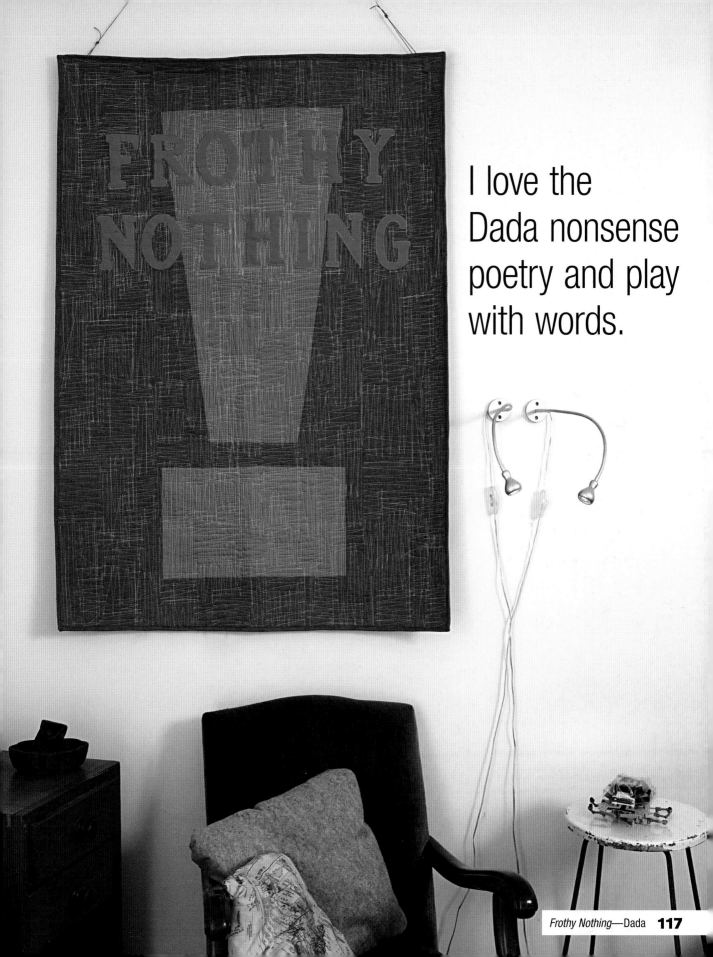

I love the Dada nonsense poetry and play with words.

PIECING

1. Lay one of the 5¼″ × 32″ background strips along the long cut edge of the red wedge-shaped piece. Line up the edges, sew, and press. Repeat for the other side. Trim to make a 17″ × 28″ rectangle.

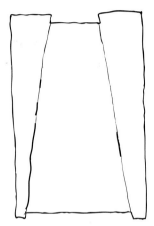

2. Sew the 2½″ × 17″ background strip onto the bottom edge of the piece from Step 1 and press. Add the red rectangle and press. This is the center panel.

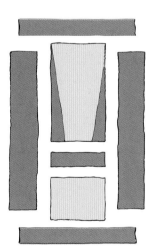

3. Attach the 10″-wide background strips onto the sides of the center panel and then the 5″-wide strips to the bottom and the top. Press the entire quilt top.

APPLIQUÉ LETTERING

1. Find a font you like. Either download one from an online font website (like dafont.com) or use a standard font from your computer.

2. Using your word processing program, type the word you want and enlarge it until you get the size you want. My letters are approximately 3″–4″ wide and 5″ tall.

> **Caution:** Letters traced on the paper side of fusible web will result in backward letters on your quilt.

3. Trace the symmetrical letters you need onto the paper side of your fusible web.

For the letters that need a mirror image, trace them first onto the glue side of the fusible webbing; then flip it over and hold it up to a window, and retrace the mirror image onto the paper side of the webbing.

 TIP If you are using a font from a website or a word processing program, there is no need to waste paper printing the letters. Instead, hold your piece of fusible web directly against the computer screen and trace the letters with a pencil.

4. Roughly cut around the letters and then fuse to the wrong side of the fabric following the manufacturer's instructions. Carefully cut out the letters with a pair of small sharp scissors.

5. Remove the paper backing and lay the letters out on your quilt top. Use a ruler to make sure the words are level and evenly spaced. Pin them in place.

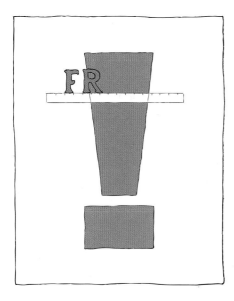

6. When you are happy with the placement, fuse them in place following the manufacturer's instructions. Sew around the outside of the letters with a small zigzag stitch.

FINISHING

1. Create a backing and batting 4″ larger than the quilt top on all sides.

For the backing on this quilt, I used upholstery-weight fabric to give the wallhanging more substance.

2. Baste, quilt, and bind your quilt (see Finishing the Quilt, page 145). This quilt was machine quilted using a freestyle-scribble improvised design.

Design Your Own

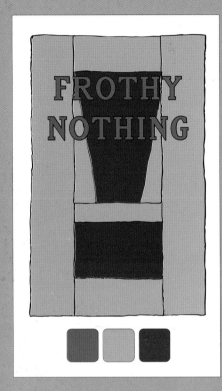

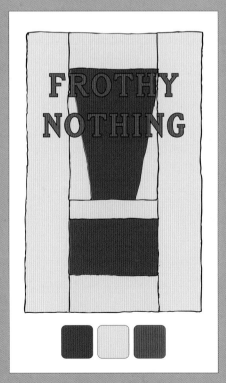

I really had a lot of fun with this quilt. Since the background is pretty straightforward, you can go all out with the appliqué text. Cover an entire quilt top with an inspiring quote or poem; use words from one of the Dada manifestos (you can find these online), lyrics from a favorite song, or a piece from a favorite novel.

I love fonts and typography, and you can personalize this quilt using your favorite font—again, many can be found online. Using this method of tracing a font onto fusible web and appliquéing it onto the fabric allows you to replicate complicated fonts quite accurately. Go all out and experiment with handwriting fonts, stenciled fonts, or fonts with wonderfully intricate curls.

I think this quilt is best kept to a simple color palette; this allows the words to speak without interruption. Try some other old-fashioned letterpress ink colors; faded-paper yellow and pink or black and green would work just as well as those shown here.

You can personalize this quilt using your favorite font.

BREAK THE RULES

The punk scene in the 1970s and 80s was all about breaking the rules, thinking outside the traditional box. It was a music and fashion underground movement, with slogans like "Good is boring," "No future," "Ugly is beautiful," and "Loud Fast Rules!"

Bands like the Sex Pistols and the Ramones set the scene for shocking lyrics and grungy DIY fashion. This underground DIY movement—where street-smart music fans refashioned their clothes, put safety pins through everything, and re-mixed traditions like tartan fabric and the Union Jack (English flag)—was not afraid of going against the grain. Colors were high-contrast acid green, hot pink, electric yellow, and red and black. The punk fashion and musical lyrics shocked and disturbed the senses.

This loud, brash, rebel quilt takes many of these aspects, like tartan fabric, breaking-the-rules ethos, and grungy and acidic colors, to create a fun, rule-breaking wallhanging quilt. *Break the Rules* is a quilt with personality. I decided to embrace freestyle wonky lines and harsh and dirty colors to create this "Ugly is beautiful" homage to the punk-style Union Jack. You'll either love it or hate it, but either way you can't ignore it.

FASHION

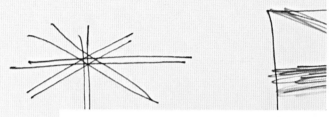

text
graffiti

Quilt size: 66½″ × 42½″, wall quilt

Finished block size: 33″ × 21″

Difficulty: Medium

Techniques: Improvised, sewn blocks and stenciled text

Break
The
Rules

Make-Do

COLOR PALETTE

Punk colors are loud, brash, and extreme—a lot of black and gray, mixed with bloody reds, acid-wash green, electric yellow, and shocking pink.

I used few colors in this quilt but many fabrics and textures. The background is a scrap patchwork of grungy gray fabrics—stripes and tartans (plaid). The center panel is a slightly textured charcoal fabric (also used in the binding), while the stripes are a mixture of green and yellow, red, a sturdy blue, and light gray. I used a combination of solids, stripes, and tartans to complete the look.

Materials

Background scrap patchwork: ⅜ yard each (3 yards total) of 8 gray fabrics (raid the scrap bin or chop up some tartan clothing.)

Red: ½ yard

Deep blue: ¼ yard

Acid green: ¼ yard

Yellow: ¼ yard

Light gray: ¼ yard

Charcoal gray: ¼ yard for the center panel

Backing: 3 yards

Binding: ½ yard to match your center panel

Batting: 74″ × 50″

Freezer paper and craft knife

Fabric paint and sponge (white or fluorescent pink or green)

Fusible web: approximately 20″ × 20″

Butcher paper or copy paper (*optional*)

Break the Rules

You'll either love it or hate it.

PIECING

1. If you have a design wall, use some masking tape to create a rectangle 33″ × 21″. Mask lines leading from one corner to the other and then fanning out to the edges; you'll need about 10 lines. If you don't have a design wall, draw this rectangle with lines fanning out onto a piece of paper. You'll use this as a guide only to keep you on track as you are improvising your block. Mark the areas for the gray scrap patchwork.

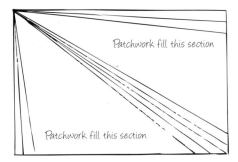

Note

You won't precut any of the fabrics. Cut as you go, working intuitively and improvisationally.

2. Cut strips as you need them and piece the background grays together, scrap-patchwork style, to create 4 large pieces of fabric approximately 40″ × 22″.

3. Place one of these pieces onto your block guide where you have marked the scrap-patchwork sections. Use your guide to mark and then cut 2 triangle wedge shapes and fit them onto your block guide (make sure to include enough overhang fabric about 1″ on all sides for seam allowances and room for error).

4. Cut 2½″-wide strips for the top 3 or 4 angled lines, or if you don't want too many strips, you can make them a bit wider. Place these onto the block guide at the top. Lay the first strip against the next strip to create your angled line, pin in place, and sew. There is no need to trim before sewing. Trim the bulk from the seam after sewing and press the seam in one direction.

5. Repeat Step 4 to sew the next couple of strips in the same way, alternating color choices and mixing up the width of the strips as you like.

6. Attach the first gray scrap-patchwork wedge.

7. Cut and sew the next set of strips, then add the next gray scrap-patchwork wedge, and continue to add the final set of strips.

Yes, it will be bulky at the corner, but trimming the seams as you go and pressing all in one direction will help.

8. Trim the blocks to 33½″ × 21½″.

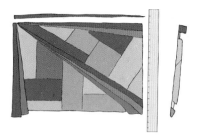

 TIP The corners do not have to be perfectly aligned; these will be covered by your center text panel.

9. Make another block the same as the previous one, following Steps 1–8. Then create a second version of your paper block guide from Step 1 with the angle going from the opposite corner. Make 2 more blocks using this new guide and Steps 1–8.

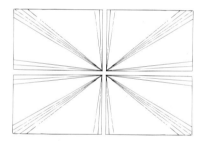

10. Sew the 4 blocks together.

 TIP The center section is now going to be super bulky. Press it into submission with a steam iron.

STENCILED TEXT

1. Using a stencil font (from a font site like dafont.com), size your text up to 3″ high on your computer and then print it or follow the tip on page 118 to trace from your computer screen instead of printing (you could photocopy a font you like from a magazine or draw one yourself, too).

2. Trace your letters onto the dull side of freezer paper. I have used the phrase "Break the Rules," but you could write anything you like. Try some of those punk phrases I mentioned on page 122, or try something contemporary from a song you like or a popular saying.

TIP → Freezer paper is slightly waxy on one side. When this side is ironed onto fabric, it sticks quite firmly but is easily removed without leaving any residue, making it perfect for stencils.

3. Cut out your freezer-paper stenciled letters carefully using a craft knife and cutting mat. These letters will be used to mask the fabric; you will be painting the frame around the letter, rather than the letter itself. Place these letters on your charcoal fabric background, leaving a 2½″–3½″ space between each letter, and fuse them in place with your hot iron.

4. Cut out strips of freezer paper and place them around your fused letter, creating a frame around each letter. This is the section you'll be painting. Iron the freezer paper strips in place. Use extra freezer paper to protect the areas of your fabric that you don't wish to paint.

Freezer-paper strips and letters

5. Using a small sponge brush or piece of a kitchen sponge, dab a little fabric paint in a contrasting color, like fluorescent green or white, and fill in the space around your letters. Paint 3 to 5 thin coats, letting the paint dry between coats. When you are happy with the coverage and the paint has fully dried, remove the freezer-paper letters and masking strips and heat set the fabric paint with a warm iron following the manufacturer's instructions.

Fabric paint around letters

6. Cut out your letter panels to the size you require and fuse your fusible web to the wrong side of this fabric. Next, remove the paper backing and position the panels in the center of your quilt. If you are using more than one piece, position them all at once, overlapping them as you like. Then when you are happy with the position, iron them in place.

7. Machine stitch around the edges of the pieces using a bold zigzag stitch.

FINISHING

1. Create a backing and batting 4″ larger than the quilt top on all sides.

For the backing on this quilt I chose to use a very sturdy tartan fabric.

2. Baste, quilt, and bind your quilt (see Finishing the Quilt, page 145). This quilt was machine quilted using a freestyle improvised design.

Design Your Own

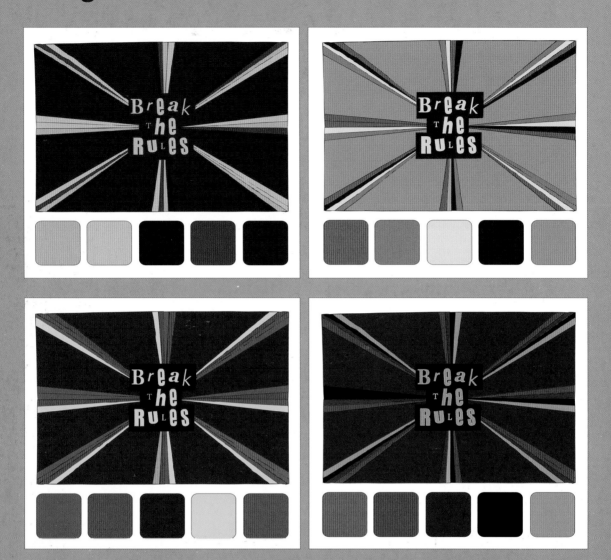

This quilt has a few elements that you can mix and match to make it your own: line, color, and text.

Text is an obvious way to customize this quilt: change the font, the words, or the scale of the letters.

Naturally, changing the colors and fabrics would alter this quilt dramatically. Using only solid colors and a simple charcoal background would simplify the design, making it quite stylish; using wider and less angular strips would simplify it even further.

If you like the visual impact of this quilt but hate wonky lines and improvised sewing, you can always use the block guide you drew as a foundation paper template and create perfect angles and lines using foundation piecing. Of course, that would go against everything that is punk, so ...

I urge you to throw caution to the wind and try it improv style!

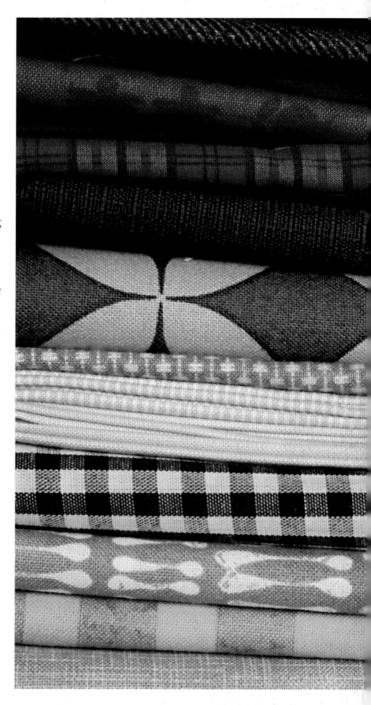

SO WHAT

Pop art was just one part of a whole social movement that incorporated art, culture, fashion, and music. Pop art was ironic—poking fun at consumerist society, at politics, and at itself—while celebrating the everyday, the expendable, and the mass-produced. It was vivid and alive; the shapes and designs were striking yet simple, and their repetition was part of the consumption. Leading this art movement were artists Andy Warhol, famous for his Elvis Presley, Marilyn Monroe, and *Campbell's Soup Cans* prints; Roy Lichtenstein, known for his cartoon paintings; and Jasper Johns, known for his American flag paintings. Their ironic use of everyday icons epitomized this whole era. Andy Warhol is no doubt the best-known artist from this era, known as much for his art as for the things he said. He was constantly quoted—"15 minutes of fame" is credited to him.

So What is a pretty quilt—pretty circles and pretty fabrics arranged with lovely symmetry. It has those pop art elements of repetition and simple shapes and bright colors. The text brings in an element of irony—making you question the context of the quilt and the intention of the maker—I like that!

POP

r culture

Repetition

SO WHAT !

WHAAM

Quilt size: 44″ × 44″, wall quilt

Difficulty: Medium

Techniques: Crazy quilting, foundation piecing, and machine appliqué

Materials

Circles: Scraps of 7 different color groupings (orange, pink, yellow, green, blue, purple, and gray)

Background: 2½ yards of white (or light gray)—this will include enough extra for the binding

Letters: Scraps of dark gray

Backing: 3 yards

Binding: ½ yard, if you don't want to use the background fabric

Batting: 52″ × 52″

Copy paper or foundation piecing paper: enough for 7 circles about 13″ in diameter and 6 letters about 4″ × 4″ each

Fusible web: enough for 7 circles about 11″ in diameter

Cutting

➜ 2″–6″-long pieces of scraps, enough to cover your circle, somewhere between 10 and 15 scraps per color

➜ One piece 24½″ × 44″ and two pieces 10½″ × 44″ piece of background fabric; the remaining length can be used to cut your binding strips

Pop art embraced irony and kitsch and didn't take itself too seriously.

PIECING SCRAPPY CIRCLES

1. Draw an 11″-diameter circle onto foundation paper using a compass and pencil, or trace around a dinner plate (this is the front of the foundation).

2. Cut around the circle leaving 1″ extra around the edge.

3. Place your first patch on the back of the foundation paper, in the center of your circle, with the right side facing up.

4. Lay your next piece right side down on the first piece, lining up one edge (Figure A). Sew this edge, then flip it over and press it down. Then fold the paper back along the seamline and trim the seam allowance (Figure B). Continue working around your center piece, repeating this process until the circle is filled (Figures C and D). Occasionally you may piece scraps together first and then add them to the foundation as a unit.

TIP Place your ironing board near your sewing machine for convenient pressing.

5. Press it all nice and neat, and then flip the paper over to your drawn circle side and carefully cut out the circle shape.

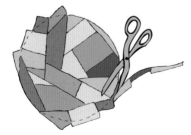

6. Repeat Steps 1–5 with your other 5 bright-colored scrappy circles.

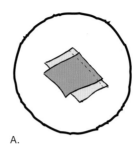
A.

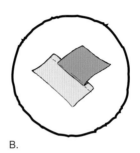
B.

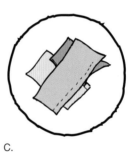
C.

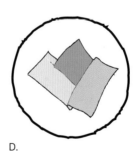
D.

TEXT

For the center circle, the first step is to foundation piece the letters.
Copy the patterns onto foundation paper with 185% enlargement.

1. Grab a scrap and cut it ¼″ larger on all sides than you need for the first section. Using a ¼″ ruler is really handy, or you can estimate. When you hold your pattern piece up to the light, you'll see the fabric extending around all sides of the section.

2. Check the size and trim the next piece in the same way. Place the right sides together with the edges lined up where you are sewing, making sure that the edges have a ¼″ seam allowance. Pin or hold these 2 fabrics in place and take them to the machine. Stitch on the paper side along the line, with the fabric underneath.

 Use a shorter stitch length than usual so that it will be easier to tear the paper away at the end.

3. Fold back the paper along the line you just sewed and use a ruler (¼″ ruler if you have one) and rotary cutter to trim the excess fabric in the seam allowance. Fold piece number 2 up into position and press into place.

4. Repeat Steps 2 and 3 with the remaining pieces. If your letter has a couple of sections that need to be foundation pieced separately, do these and then sew the sections together to create your letter.

5. After you have made all your letters, press them and tear the paper away from the back. Then arrange them over your last foundation circle. Crazy patch these to your circle, filling in the spaces with scrap fabric (again you can piece scraps together to create units before sewing them onto your foundation), using the same flip-and-sew method as before in Piecing Scrappy Circles (page 136).

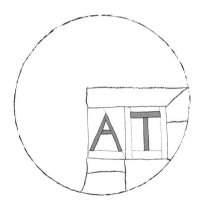

6. When you have sewn all the letters and your circle is filled, press, then turn over the fabric to the paper back, and trim around the circle.

ASSEMBLY

1. Remove the paper from the back of the circles and then fuse the fusible web onto the back of all the circle pieces.

2. Take the square of background fabric and place it onto your design wall, or lay it out somewhere flat. Find the center point, and place your text circle right in the middle. Then arrange your crazy patch circles around it, getting the spacing about 1″–2″ apart.

3. When you have your spacing right and you are happy with the position of the circles, fuse them in place following the manufacturer's instructions.

4. Sew around the outside edge of the circles, using a zigzag stitch to secure them in place.

FINISHING

1. Create a backing and batting 4″ larger than the quilt top on all sides.

For the backing on this quilt, I used a pretty floral vintage fabric.

2. Baste, quilt, and bind your quilt (see Finishing the Quilt, page 145). This quilt was machine quilted using a freestyle improvised design.

Design Your Own

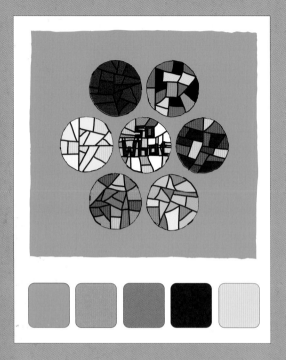

Because this quilt has lots of fun aspects, it is easily customizable. Color is an obvious choice—go fluorescent, go pastel, go rainbow! My color variations include a masculine color palette in various shades and a baby color palette in pastels.

Shape is another way to vary this quilt—think triangles or big hexagons, and of course you can change the entire flavor of a quilt with different background fabrics. I love white with this quilt because it sets off the colors so prettily, but you could go more dramatic with charcoal, or make it a baby quilt and use peach or pale blue.

I think the main way to personalize this quilt is through the text that you use. You can leave out the text altogether if you like, or make it your own. "So What" could be changed to another Andy Warhol quote like, "I like boring things" or "I want to be plastic." Or use something your teenage kids might say, like, "Whatever" or "Who Cares."

And you don't have to be ironic, sardonic, or aloof, of course—be kitschy, bitchy, or funny instead. You might want to consult the Urban Dictionary online (urbandictionary.com)—it's an eye-opener!

You can leave out the text altogether if you like, or make it your own.

YOUR TOOLBOX

The Basics

SEWING MACHINE

Sewing quilts requires a sewing machine—unless you like to hand sew all your quilts. I'm going to go right ahead and assume that you are mostly using a sewing machine.

For my main sewing I use a very simple mid-range machine. It has a few fancy stitches but is basically a sturdy, solid newish machine. I have a good relationship with my local sewing machine repair shop and dealer and take my machine in for a service once a year. Between those yearly service visits, I make sure to care for my machine by cleaning and oiling it regularly.

I have a second sewing machine. Actually it now belongs to my daughter, and it once belonged to my nanna—so it has really served us well. I learned to sew on that machine and love its sturdy reliability.

SEWING MACHINE ACCESSORIES

Along with your sewing machine you'll need a free-motion foot (a darning or embroidery foot) and perhaps a walking foot, and of course, appropriate sewing needles and threads too—I use standard sewing needles and a good-quality cotton thread in neutral tones: white, gray, and parchment.

Make sure you have a manual for your machine so that you are familiar with its capabilities and know how to troubleshoot any issues. You need to have a good understanding of how the tension works and how to lower the feed dogs so you can do free-motion quilting.

BEFORE-SEWING CHECKLIST

Before starting work on a new project I always make sure to fill a few bobbins with neutral thread, clean and oil my machine, pop in a new needle if I haven't changed it in a while, do a tension check, adjust my lighting, and make sure I am comfortable. Nearby, I keep some snipping scissors, a pincushion, and my seam ripper handy.

CUTTING

For cutting purposes I have three good scissors that are forbidden to leave my sewing room: small, sharp scissors for clipping seams and threads; my good old fabric scissors; and a pair of utility scissors for paper, plastic, and such.

I have a couple of rotary cutters and make sure to change the blades when they begin to feel dull. I also have a self-healing cutting mat and a few different cutting rulers such as a 5″ square ruler, a 10″ square ruler, a 2½″-wide straight ruler, and a ¼″ ruler. The right ruler is a very handy time-saving device that ensures accurate cutting.

My cutting bench is at waist height—like a kitchen bench. This saves my back. I also have set up my sewing machine on this bench too—as I have found that I like to stand while sewing. My ironing board and cutting mat are right there too, which makes the sew, press, and trim sequence extremely efficient.

IRON

Naturally, you'll need an iron. It's almost as important when quilting as your sewing machine! Keep it nearby. I don't use an ironing board; instead I have a thick, folded towel set up on the bench behind me. My space is not large enough for an extra piece of furniture.

More Gadgets

Apart from fabric, thread, a sewing machine, iron, your cutting tools, and your basic sewing kit, what else do you need for quiltmaking? The short answer is not much else, really. But the long answer is that there are so many helpful and interesting sewing and quilting gadgets available that it is very easy to get lost and confused.

Here is my very basic list, the things you will need to make the quilts in this book; but available products for quilting are nearly endless. Just go to your local quilt store to browse, and don't forget to read the manufacturer's directions before using.

QUILTING

If you are going to hand quilt, you'll need a quilting hoop and hand-quilting needles, plus appropriate threads and a thimble. If you are machine quilting, you will need some "grippy" quilting (or garden) gloves and the correct sewing machine presser foot for your needs.

BINDING AND BASTING

Making binding is so easy—it is worth it to make your own. You should never, ever need to buy premade binding. All you really need is fabric and an iron. For basting your quilt, you can use a needle and thread, basting safety pins, or, my preference, basting spray.

APPLIQUÉ AND FOUNDATION PIECING

Making templates and patterns will require tracing paper, copy paper, freezer paper, or template plastic.

If you plan to foundation piece, you can use copy paper or fine interfacing, but you can use any lightweight paper or buy specialty papers (such as Carol Doak's Foundation Paper) for the purpose.

Fusible web is extremely handy to have if you are doing appliqué—I use it all the time. Water-soluble appliqué glue is also useful.

FINISHING THE QUILT

Assembling the Quilt

So you have finished your quilt top and are ready to quilt.

Your quilt top is the main feature of the quilt, but the other elements are pretty important, too—it wouldn't be a quilt without them. The batting provides the softness and warmth, and the backing can be either decorative or plain. The quilting holds these three layers together and makes the quilt a quilt. You can choose to hand quilt, to machine quilt at home, or to send it out to be professionally quilted. Finally, the binding finishes the edges neatly and frames the quilt.

QUILT SANDWICH

When assembling your quilt, layer your quilt top and quilt backing with your batting in between—this is called the quilt sandwich. These layers are first held together with basting before being quilted. After quilting, the edges are squared up and the binding is added to the outside edge to protect the quilt.

BATTING

You'll need some batting (wadding); this is the filler that gives loft and warmth to your quilt. There are many types of batting, and you should take into consideration what purpose the quilt will serve and how you plan to quilt it and clean it. If in doubt, ask for advice at your local quilting store.

I pretty much always use 100% cotton batting. I find it easy to work with, it's machine washable, and I love that crinkly softness it gets after washing.

TIP If you don't have one large piece of batting, you can sew your batting offcuts together to make a large usable piece. Butt the sections together and overstitch with a wide zigzag or hand sew with a tacking stitch.

BACKING

The back of your quilt can be as simple and as practical as you like, or you could make a complementary design to create a double-sided quilt. Choose fabric similar to the quilt front, as this makes washing and caring for the quilt easier.

I don't use just one type of quilt backing; I decide what is best for each quilt based on what I have on hand, how much time I have, and how motivated I am to create an interesting alter ego for my quilt. I nearly always use fabric from my stash: complementary fabrics, leftover scraps, vintage fabrics, feature prints, and sometimes vintage sheets, too. I often make an improvised pieced backing using a combination of large and scrap pieces.

I find that using the "rule of thirds" is helpful when creating a visually appealing yet simple quilt back. Imagine the backing as an image divided into thirds horizontally and vertically. Where the thirds intersect, you place an interesting visual element, a spare quilt block, a stripe in a different color, and so on. This creates some tension and energy.

The four quilt-backing examples shown here are the reverse sides of four of the quilts in this book. I used scraps and improvisational-style sewing to make the most of leftover fabrics from the quilt tops with the addition of other scrap and stash fabrics. It is so very satisfying to be able to make a small dent in my scraps—and also a fun, playful way to finish after following a more structured design for the quilt top.

Neutral Play

The back of *Gray Play* (page 80), a structured, simple quilt front that plays with color, is a freer design, which I call "Neutral Play." It is an improvised Log Cabin design made entirely of scraps from my neutrals—with a few dusky yellows and blues thrown in to catch the eye. The design is a 3 × 3 layout. I just kept adding to the blocks until they were the size I wanted, and then I trimmed them square to sew them together.

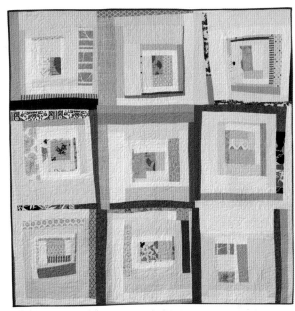

Gray Play, back

Highway

On the opposite side of *Intersections* (page 40) is "Highway," three wide, improvised strips made of a mixture of dark and medium gray prints, textures, and solids. These are contained within a light gray sashing and a border to bring some order to the chaos.

To make this sort of improvisational design, first, measure your quilt and divide it into thirds. This is the width of your improvisational strips. Then, begin by making improvised slab pieces using fairly large scraps and build them up by adding pieces until you get the width you require. Sew these pieces into strips until you get the length you require. Sew these together with a neutral sashing and add a border if required.

Intersections, back

Blue Windows

The reverse side of *Peacock Blue* (page 98) has an off-center section of framed scrappy blocks, "Blue Windows," with the remaining area made from some precious soft linen. The off-center panel is made from crazily patchworked small- to medium-sized scraps left over from the quilt front, which are then trimmed into 10″-wide blocks, sashed with a neutral gray, and sewn together in a panel.

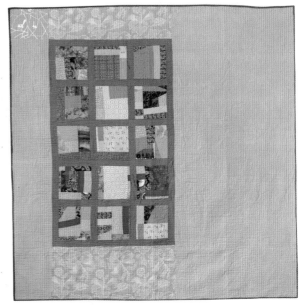

Peacock Blue, back

Accidental Color

I think I had the most fun making the back of *Clear Cut* (page 72). I rummaged in my solid-colored scraps and smaller stash pieces to make it random and improvised. It is made from a mixture of improvised scrap slabs, large scraps, and small pieces sewn first into rectangular slabs and then into colorful strips of different widths, which are then sewn together. This backing has a structure in the strips but enough random elements—different widths and mixed-up scrappy "Accidental Color" slabs—to make you surprised and happy each time you look at it.

Clear Cut, back

WHEN CHOOSING A QUILT BACK, KEEP THESE TIPS IN MIND

→ Choose fabric with a depth of color similar to the quilt top. This makes it easier to match the thread in the bobbin and on the spool, and therefore prevents "freckles" of high-contrast thread showing through your quilt.

→ If you are quilting for the first time, consider using a busy print to hide less-than-perfect quilting stitches.

→ Your backing should be 4″–5″ wider than the quilt top all around (especially if you are sending the quilt out to be quilted on a longarm machine). This gives some leeway for squaring up your quilt sandwich when your quilting is complete.

→ Press seams open on your backing to ensure that it lies flat.

LAYERING AND BASTING

Basting is pretty much the bane of any quilter's life—the least-liked step in the quilting process (although some quilters profess to love this step), but still very necessary. Proper basting prevents quilting stitches from puckering and the quilt layers from misaligning.

I have a longarm quilting machine now (the best secondhand buy ever), so I can skip the basting step. If you plan to send your quilt out to be professionally quilted or if you have your own quilting machine and quilting frame, then you can skip this step too (hurrah!).

Before purchasing my longarm quilting machine, I used basting spray to baste my quilts. Seriously, you have to try it, unless you are hand quilting (in which case stick to the other methods, because the glue is likely to gum up your needle). It is more effective than pins or stitching at holding the layers together, but there are some precautions you need to take.

Getting Ready to Baste

1. Spread your quilt backing right side down onto a large flat surface. Use masking tape to secure the edges so that it doesn't move. The tension should be even all across the backing cloth.

2. Place the batting on top of the backing. Then place your quilt top, with the right side facing up, centered over the batting and smooth it out. Check to be sure your backing and batting are about 4″ larger than the quilt top on all sides.

Pin and Stitch Basting

Both pin and stitch basting require you to begin in the center and work your way out to each edge, pinning (use basting pins) or stitching (use long tacking stitches) approximately every 6″.

Spray Basting

Be sure to use a good-quality basting spray from your quilting store and use it in a well-ventilated space.

1. Tape your quilt backing down and secure it with masking tape; then layer the batting on top.

2. Roll the batting carefully onto a wide length of dowel (or a broomstick with the broom removed), all the way to one end without lifting, so that when it is rolled back it stays aligned (Figure A).

3. Spray the adhesive lightly over the backing fabric and unroll the batting onto the sticky backing a little at a time, smoothing as you go.

4. Repeat Steps 2 and 3 with the quilt top. Then lift your quilt and turn it over, smoothing the backing down one last time.

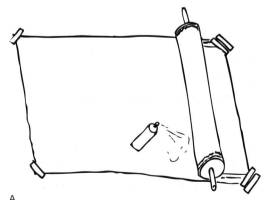

A.

Quilting

The quilting is those lovely stitches that hold the layers together. Sturdy and practical and decorative, the quilting provides the structure, texture, and subtle beauty of the finished quilt.

If you decide to hand quilt, I applaud you. The special quality of hand quilting cannot be duplicated by machine. If you don't have the time to hand quilt the whole quilt, you could add some hand-stitched elements for a special touch. None of the quilts in this book are hand quilted, so I am not including directions here. You can find plenty of online tutorials or specialty books on the subject.

Machine quilting is more my thing. It is quick and utilitarian, but not as easy as you might think. It takes skill and patience to get the stitches even and to prevent the fabric from puckering. If you are machine quilting on your home sewing machine, you should ensure you are comfortable and have good lighting and a good chair, as it will take a while.

The two methods of machine quilting that I use are stitching in straight lines and free-motion quilting. With each method you can create different designs, and you will need a special presser foot for your sewing machine.

MACHINE-QUILTING METHODS

Straight-Line Quilting

When you are stitching grids or lines, use a walking foot. It "walks" the top layer of fabric, while the bottom layer moves along with the feed dogs. This helps ensure that the top layer stays put and doesn't pull more or less than the bottom layer.

With straight-line quilting, it's a good idea to have a guide to keep your lines parallel. You could mark your entire quilt top using a ruler and masking tape or dissolvable fabric markers, or you could use a guide arm that attaches to your sewing machine. Either way requires you to be patient and take your time. Why not listen to some crafty podcasts while you sew those seemingly endless straight lines.

Stitching in straight lines doesn't have to be boring. Why not try some simple horizontal straight lines, or crisscross design, or even outline stitches. I like very, very dense straight-line quilting, too.

CHECKLIST FOR QUILTING BY MACHINE

➜ Clean and oil your machine, start with a fresh needle, and fill several bobbins.

➜ Check your tension on a small sample of fabric and batting similar to what's in your quilt, and practice your quilting design.

➜ Check to be sure that you have the correct foot on your machine and you have lowered the feed dogs, if you need to.

➜ When you stop, make sure you keep the needle down in the fabric to ensure there are no breaks in your design.

➜ Begin stitching in the center of the quilt and smooth out the area you will quilt first to prevent puckering.

Free-Motion Quilting

Free-motion quilting (a rambling allover design) can be planned or improvised. Lower your sewing machine's feed dogs and use a free-motion foot, which will skim lightly across the fabric surface and prevent skipped stitches.

When you sew with the feed dogs down, you control the stitch length by the speed with which you move the fabric; this means that you need to have a good grip on the fabric—which is where grippy quilting gloves come in very handy.

Moving the fabric at an even pace results in nice, even stitches, but this takes practice (and strong hands).

Before stitching, draw your design in a continuous line onto paper without lifting your pencil; practice getting an even density. Try some organic-shaped stones, leaves, or wood grain once you get the hang of the simple stipple designs.

Binding

I bound all the quilts in this book in the same way. I have tried all different types of binding and have finally discovered my preferred method—it is simple and neat and works perfectly every single time. Your preferred method might be completely different!

I almost always make my binding on the straight grain—unless I am binding curved corners or a wavy edge, in which case I make bias binding.

I create neat mitered corners and machine sew one side and hand sew the other. Sometimes I machine sew both sides of the binding—if I am in a hurry or if the quilt is going to be used and washed a lot—you know, if it is for a baby or a child.

I use binding that either contrasts with and frames the quilt or blends in and becomes almost invisible. Sometimes I break the rules and make a scrappy binding.

DOUBLE-FOLD BINDING

I always make my own binding, and I think quilters have to do this; all you need are scissors, a pencil, a ruler, and an iron—and the fabric of course. Double-fold binding has a double thickness of fabric, which gives the quilt added protection and a longer life. Square up your quilt before you add the binding.

1. Mark 2½"-wide lines from selvage to selvage on the wrong side of the fabric, using a ruler and pencil (Figure A). Then sew the selvage edges together, right sides facing, leaving an offset of one line's width (2½") and matching up all the subsequent lines when you sew (Figure B). Press the seam open.

2. Use your scissors and cut along the marked lines, beginning at the offset line (Figure C). Continue cutting along this line until you reach the end. Ta-da! You have one long strip of fabric.

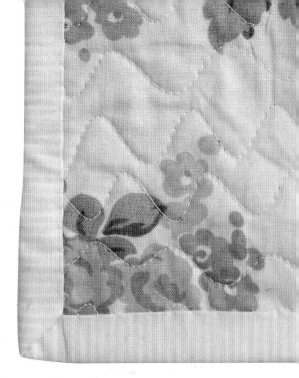

A. Mark lines selvage to selvage.

B. Leave an offset of one line's width.

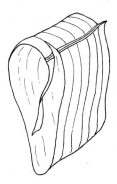

C. Cut along marked lines.

3. Press the strip in half along the length and then roll it up so it is ready to use.

4. Line up the long raw edges of the binding with the raw edges of the top of the quilt, leaving a 6″–10″ tail of binding at the beginning (Figure D).

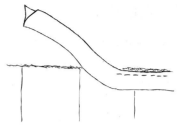

D.

5. Begin sewing through all layers, using a ¼″ seam allowance. Stop ¼″ from the corner, backstitch a couple of stitches, and remove the quilt from under the presser foot.

6. To make your mitered corner, fold the binding up and away from you at a 45° angle. Hold the angled fold in place as you fold the binding neatly back down, aligning it with the next quilt edge to be sewn (Figure E).

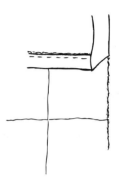

7. Begin stitching the next side at the top of the fold. Continue onto the next corner and repeat with the remaining corners (Figure F).

E.

8. When you are almost back to where you began, stop and trim the end of the binding, leaving each end with a ¼″ seam allowance (Figure G). Open up the binding and sew it together (right sides facing), finger-press the seam open, and close the binding up again (Figure H). Then place the raw edge back onto the quilt edge and finish sewing.

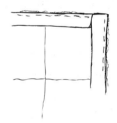

F.

9. Fold the binding over to the back of the quilt, enclosing the

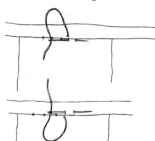

raw edge. At this point you can choose to hand sew with a ladder stitch or to machine stitch, depending upon the style of the rest of your quilt (and how much time you have).

G.

Wow, you finished making the quilt! Give yourself a pat on the back, eat some chocolate, make a cup of tea, and feel good about yourself. But wait—there are just a few more steps before you can get snuggly with that baby.

Wash the quilt and attach a label. Don't worry; it won't take long.

H.

LABELING

I recently made a whole bunch of quilt labels by uploading an image (which I designed in Photoshop) to the print-on-demand online fabric store Spoonflower.com. I ordered a yard of the fabric in cotton and designed it so that the labels are approximately 5½″ × 3½″. I recommend doing this because it's handy to have some labels on hand and, well—it's fun.

If you don't need a whole yard of labels, you have plenty of other options for labeling your quilts: embroidery, permanent fabric pens, stenciling, stamping—anything permanent will do. Make it pretty and make it yours! Don't forget to include the date.

Washing and Storing Fabric and Quilts

I rarely wash my fabric before sewing with it. There is simply too much! And, I don't have the time. There are exceptions—batiks and hand dyes, reds, blues, and purples—especially if I am planning on mixing them with a white background. But for the most part I don't wash fabrics before sewing, but I do wash my quilts after I have quilted them. (There are risks involved in this method, and I have been caught once before!)

Washing quilts for me is a fairly simple business. Because I use only cotton or linen fabric and only cotton batting, I can safely wash my quilts in the washing machine. I use a gentle cycle, cold water, and a small amount of ecofriendly detergent. I then either dry them on the line in a gentle breeze or pop them in the dryer on the

gentle cycle. The small amount of shrinkage that occurs in the dryer gives them a pleasant crinkly texture that I love.

My fabrics are stored away from harsh sunlight. Light can and will fade fabrics, so be careful if your shelving is near a window. I like to store my fabrics in color order. Not only is it pleasing to look upon those piles of color-coded fabrics, but it also makes finding fabrics for your color scheme much simpler.

Storing your quilts is a different matter and can be quite tricky—especially if you are getting a bit of a collection going! I have a quilt on every bed, of course, and on the couches and walls, too! The rest of them rotate in and out of storage in a linen bag in a dry, dark cupboard.

USING YOUR QUILTS

I don't need to tell you how to use your quilt. What is there to know? Snuggle up with your loved ones on the couch and read a book or watch a show. You can attach a hanging sleeve or some little fabric loops to the back of the quilt, thread a length of dowel through, and hang it on your wall. You can sling that quilt over your tired couch and add some color to your room.

Display your everyday quilts in a folded stack on the sideboard—or store them away in a dry, dark cupboard, rolled up and out of the way. Whether your quilts are in storage, on display, or in use, make sure to rotate them often and shake them out and air them out on the line every now and again.

Appendix

METRIC CONVERSION

As an Australian quilter I need to be familiar with the metric and the imperial measuring systems. I use an online metric conversion calculator (such as unitednotions.com/metric_calculator.html or onlineconversion.com). Here are some standard measurements in both metric and imperial units:

¼″ (common seam allowance) = 0.64cm

2½″ (common binding strip width) = 6.4cm

5″ (charm square size) = 12.7cm

10″ (layer cake size) = 25.5cm

12″ (a common basic block size) = 30.5cm

1 yard of fabric = 36″ or 91cm

1 meter of fabric = 39⅜″ or 1⅛ yards

44″ (common quilting fabric width) = 1.12 meters

CALCULATING YARDAGE

Yardage is calculated for you in the quilt projects in this book, based on 40″-wide fabric, with an additional ⅛ yard to allow for error. If you are going to alter the quilt sizes or if you are using a different width of fabric, you will need to recalculate how much fabric you will need. Some excellent resources online can help you calculate your fabric backing, binding, and even borders (see Resources, page 159).

Patterns

Triangle pattern for *Sublime Triangle*

Diamond pattern for Bright Future

Feather motif pattern for *Blue Peacock*

Resources

I am a blog and online craft junkie. Lots of resources, tutorials, websites, and stores can be found online to keep you engrossed every single minute of the day. Here are few of my favorites.

Quilting Blogs and Websites

annamariahorner.blogspot.com

crazymomquilts.blogspot.com

handmadebyalissa.com

ohfransson.com

redpepperquilts.com

filminthefridge.com

fatquarterly.com

oliveandollie.com

cauchycomplete.wordpress.com

themodernquiltguild.com

moderndayquilts.tumblr.com

tallgrassprairiestudio.blogspot.com

stitchindye.blogspot.com

General Craft Blogs

whipup.net

trueup.net

purlbee.com

etsy.com/blog

Art and Design Inspiration

bloesem.blogs.com

thedesignfiles.net

decor8blog.com

abeautifulmess.typepad.com

poppytalk.blogspot.com

pinterest.com

Some of My Favorite Books

Quilts Made Modern, Weeks Ringle and Bill Kerr, C&T Publishing, 2010

Quilting from Little Things, Sarah Fielke, Murdoch Books, 2011

Modern Quilts, Traditional Inspiration: 20 New Designs with Historic Roots, Denyse Schmidt, STC Craft, 2012

Quilt History Books

The Quilts of Gee's Bend, William Arnett, Alvia Wardlaw, Jane Livingston, and John Beardsley, Tinwood Books, 2002

The Amish Quilt, Eve Wheatcroft Granick, Good Books, 1989

Quilts 1700–2010: Hidden Histories, Untold Stories, Sue Prichard, V&A Publishing, 2010

The American Quilt: A History of Cloth and Comfort 1750–1950, Roderick Kiracofe and Mary Elizabeth Johnson, Clarkson Potter, 2004

About the Author

Kathreen Ricketson (1971–2013) lived in Canberra, Australia, with her husband, two children, and various chooks and ducks. She spent her days alternating between running chaotically and calmly while mothering, making, and being. She loved fabric, crochet, books, cooking, camping, sewing, drawing, her children, and lots of other things besides.

She started blogging in 2004, fresh out of art school with a couple of little kids in tow, before starting Whipup.net in 2006. During 2007 she wrote a regular ecocraft and ecolifestyle column for Treehugger.com, and in 2010 she wrote a semiregular craft column for Australia's *Woman's Day* magazine. In 2012 she began a regular column for *Australian Quilters Companion* magazine, and she used to be the designer at *Art Monthly Australia* magazine. More recently, she had been writing, editing, designing, and publishing an e-magazine for kids.

Kathreen is the author of *Whip Up Mini Quilts* (Chronicle 2010) and *Little Bits Quilting Bee* (Chronicle 2011) and the editor of the *Kids' Crafternoon* series of books (Hardie Grant 2011).

Kathreen died May 15, 2013. She was fulfilling a dream of traveling the country with her family.